TREASURE
under your feet

TREASURE
under your feet

ADVENTURERS' HANDBOOK OF METAL DETECTING

BY ROY VOLKER AND DICK RICHMOND

HENRY REGNERY COMPANY • CHICAGO

Library of Congress Cataloging in Publication Data

Volker, Roy.
  Treasure under your feet.

  Includes bibliographical references.
  1. Treasure-trove. I. Richmond, Dick, joint
author. II. Title.
G525.V58   622'.19   74-23381

Copyright © 1974 by Roy Volker and Dick Richmond
All rights reserved
Published by Henry Regnery Company
180 North Michigan Avenue, Chicago, Illinois 60601
Manufactured in the United States of America
Library of Congress Catalog Card Number: 74-23381
International Standard Book Number: 0-8092-8235-6 (cloth)
                                    0-8092-8234-8 (paper)

This book is dedicated to the late Kip Wagner,
the greatest treasure finder of them all.

Contents

1
Gold in the Wake of a Storm

Working for a newspaper, a writer gets into some unusual stories. One of those that seemed as if it would be a drag turned out to be a turning point for me. It was the day I met Roy Volker.

Roy was the star attraction at a coin show at the Gateway Hotel in St. Louis a few years ago, and I was looking for a feature article. When I went, I didn't really hold much hope for anything turning out. It was just that I had nothing better to do.

Big, friendly, and easy to talk to, Roy stood out in the midst of the individuals who had set up booths for the show. All by himself he's impressive, but at the time I was more impressed by the five-pound cakes of silver, the hundreds of old Spanish gold and silver coins and the other artifacts he had picked from the bones of shipwrecks in the waters of Florida, South America, and the Caribbean.

Then he told me that the things he had on display were only a small part of his collection. He had a museum filled with items he had found, and he invited me to come see it.

The museum was in nearby Clarksville, Missouri. In it, Roy had displays of jade and jewelry, pots and bones, coins and weapons, and so many other things that I could scarcely believe one man had found it all. The exhibit was magnificent, and, even as inexperienced as I was at the time, I knew that I was looking at a fortune.

I did a feature on Roy for the paper; it was while I was working on it that we became friends. He told me about an expedition that he would be leading into Bahamian waters a few months later and invited me to come along. He was searching for *Nuestra Señora de la Maravillas*, a fabulously wealthy ship that sank on Little Bahama Bank in a storm in 1656.

Up to that time Roy had been shy about publicity. He had been featured in a number of articles in small newspapers and magazines, but nothing of any consequence. When my story about him appeared, he suddenly became prominent, and it really bugged him.

He complained that his telephone hadn't stopped ringing since the article appeared. Then suddenly his tune changed. One of the callers wanted to buy his collection — all of it.

So, before we departed on our first expedition together, Roy was out of the museum business, which frankly didn't suit him anyway.

I hadn't thought about treasure hunting before that trip. Even after seeing all the things Roy had found, the idea seemed more like fantasy than reality. My ideas were to alter, however, and radically. What did it was an introduction to electronic search equipment.

Roy is a wizard with the proton magnetometer, an instrument that detects gradients in the earth's magnetic field caused by concentrations of ferrous material such as that from a shipwreck. Day after day he found cannons and anchors and the remains of entire wrecks. The ships were really there, and the magnetometer would locate them even if they were buried.

It was during this time that the idea for a full-length motion picture about treasure hunting occurred to me. The potential seemed excellent. This wouldn't be some fictional story about mythical riches. What I was seeing on that trip were real men after real ships who were swimming in the midst of damn real sharks, barracudas, and moray eels in order to work them.

During his years as a full-time professional, Roy had filmed a lot of places he had been and worked. His film wasn't bad considering the equipment with which he was working, but it wasn't good enough to use for theaters. What it did provide were examples of what could be filmed underwater and above.

Roy's feelings about a movie project were different from mine, but I'll let him tell it.

● ● ●

When Dick approached me about his idea for a movie, we were sitting on the bow of the 79-foot diving boat *Arto*. It was near sunset, and we were anchored in shallow water off an uninhabited desert island. The crystal water glistened and the island was bathed in fiery gold.

We could see the bottom, and as we talked, we watched schools of fish move in toward a small reef in the cove. The reef almost crawled out of the water and onto the island. Suddenly the fin of a shark cut the water, and I had to grin when I caught the expression on Dick's face. He paled. Five minutes earlier he had been in the water right where the shark was now swimming.

Sharks in the Bahamas, however, are tame creatures compared to those I encountered in Ecuador several years earlier when I was there in search of a treasure. And I suspect the look on my face was pretty near that of Dick's my initial time in those waters. But that's another story.

Just being in that cove, I could understand why Dick wanted to make a motion picture. To be truthful, however, my enthusiasm for the project did not match his, at least not at first. I'm a treasure hunter, and I was after a big one. If Dick thought he could form a company that would allow me to keep searching while he was filming, that was fine with me.

In the next ten days we electronically searched several square miles of ocean floor and found the remains of twenty-eight wrecks. More than half of these were of recent vintage (circa 1800 or later), but the rest were old. From the old ones we took some interesting artifacts and some ore, which turned out to be copper. But none of the wrecks was a treasure galleon.

Suddenly, it seemed, our time was gone and we were heading back for Miami. I was taking a turn at the wheel as the rest of the hard-worked crew sprawled out on deck to take a well-deserved rest. Dick came into the cabin to tell me how sorry he was that we had not found the 1656. He knew I had been searching for that ship for a long time.

But I wasn't dissatisfied, and I said so. Over the years I had methodically combed and charted the bank until there was just a small part left to be searched. On that trip we had eliminated eighty percent of what remained. I knew my golden galleon was someplace in that remaining twenty percent.

Back in St. Louis, we immediately went to work to form the movie company. Dick and a television director took parts of the film I had shot over the years and supplemented the best of what I had with movies of paintings of galleons, ancient divers, maps, and some of my most precious finds.

Dick wrote a script and then went hustling to find things to film that would match it. A friend flew in from Paducah, Kentucky, to do the narration. Then it was all put together with music. Out of what seemed like pieces of nothing, we had a fine fifteen-minute film. It was then that I began to realize what Dick could do when he put his mind to it, and I began to appreciate the potential he kept talking about. My treasure was becoming more real to him, and his movie was starting to take on a firm reality for me. As we worked together, our ideas began to take the same direction.

Dick and I formed a partnership with three other men. The plan was to create a company to make the film and to support a two-year expedition. The film would have been shot in the first four weeks of the expedition. Other film projects would then be worked out.

Cinematographers, sound men, and other technicians were contacted, all of whom had to be divers. Motion picture exhibitors and distributors looked at the project with undisguised interest. The television director with whom Dick had been working on the short film became a diver just to direct the film. A marketing expert joined in to lend his advice and experience in the motion picture field. Insurance people were brought in. We went to extremes to make the package less of a gamble.

While Dick was doing this, I was getting everything ready for the expedition. Divers would be needed, as would a new diving boat, a good captain who was used to working with search electronics, and a demolition man. The area had to be fine charted. Nothing was going to be left undone. We weren't going to waste a penny of any investor's money with poor planning. In fact, Dick was determined not to shoot the film on a speculative basis. He had decided that we would have to have an outlet for our movie before we purchased a single roll of unexposed film. We were fully aware that many independent producers were left holding reels of film that would never be seen.

Legally it was complicated, and the partnership was a long time being prepared. When the prospectus, contracts, and everything else needed were finally completed, potential investors were contacted.

Dick and I both knew that the idea would seem like a fantasy to hard-nosed businessmen. So we were determined not only to make everything legally straight but also to offer investors something tangible to see. We had the movie short explaining what we intended to do, and I had plenty of gold and silver artifacts to show them.

Yet a motion picture project can be a gamble, too. With a treasure hunt connected to it, the prospective investors were intrigued but skeptical at first. No one could believe that known treasure could be lying on the ocean floor and still be untouched. It was a tough job of salesmanship. When the prospective investors finally started seeing enough potential in the project to pledge their money, marine archeologist Robert F. Marx found the 1656 wreck right where it had to be—in the unsearched twenty percent of my charted area.

What made the pill so hard to swallow was that this was not the first time I had come within inches of a golden galleon. A few years earlier, Mel Fisher of Treasure Salvors had offered to me for $30,000 the rights to *La Holandesa*, which went down in 1715 near Fort Pierce, Florida.

At the time, *La Holandesa* had potential, but Fisher was not completely sold on it. He needed working capital, and a contract was drawn between him and me. In those days, however, I had not established my reputation and I could not raise the money. Fisher finally worked the wreck himself and took more than $3,000,000 from it.

When the 1656 was found, Dick's disappointment was almost as great as mine. He could now tell the cautious investors how safe their money would have been, but the impetus for the combination package was gone. The movie was still a good idea. We had, however, no golden galleon to find. A film could still be made, but now the investors would regard us as if we only had half a loaf. Strange psychology, but we were stuck with it. Dick wanted to know what we were going to do next.

• • •

Three minutes after I asked the question, Roy had an answer. He knew of another wreck. For years it was assumed that one of the unfound galleons of the 1715 fleet was buried beneath the sand on a stretch of coast called Corrigan's Beach.[1] The property is owned by Hugh Corrigan, Jr., and his brother, Pat.

There are cannons in the water offshore, and for years the Corrigans have been finding coins on their beach after storms. It was a money beach and everyone knew it. However, no one had ever been able to locate a wreck.

It was assumed that if the wreck was not in the water, then it had to be on the beach. Treasure hunters wanted to work the property, but the Corrigans just were not interested in the people who came to them with various propositions.

Roy was probably the one exception. The Corrigans and he have been friends for years, and they wanted to work out an agreement with him on a dig. They finally did agree on a split, but that story is told in a later chapter. However, it was to discuss this project that we went to Florida when Roy discovered his now famous coin, the 1715 eight-escudo Spanish Golden Royal.[2]

The summer after the 1656 was uncovered, Roy and I had driven to Florida to open discussions for the Corrigan project. Roy got the negotiations started. However, it was slow going—it was late fall before we heard anything positive from Hugh.

Roy and Hugh talked by telephone, and Hugh said there were still some contract bugs to be worked out. Roy hung up and called me. He wanted us to go to Florida and iron things out with the Corrigans. The weather in St. Louis was bad and sunshine seemed like a good idea.

Before we went, we had something we had to take care of first. Roy and I were convinced that if we did get the rights to work on Corrigan's Beach, we would need the help of a civil engineer. A dig on a beach meant water; if the wreck was deep, water was going to be a problem.

1. See Chapter 20.
2. New York coin auctioneer Hans M. F. Schulman has placed a value on the Golden Royal of between $50,000 and $75,000. See Chapter 3.

Roy was itching to get going. Hugh had mentioned that the weather was starting to blow; Roy does not like flying in rough wind. But if the wind turned into a real storm, metal detecting on the beach would be great, and he wanted to be in Florida for that. When we were there that summer, Roy had taken me to some of his favorite money beaches. Many of the coins in his collection had been found in the sand after big blows. His descriptions of the things he had found then got my adrenalin going.

The day following our meeting with the civil engineer, we flew into Melbourne and were picked up at the airport by a friend with whom we would be staying.

The negotiations were quickly settled. Hugh and Pat, once they decided to go ahead with the project, were as curious as we were about what was under their beach. Hugh arranged for me to see some of the gold and silver coins that had been taken from it over the years. It was pretty exciting.

Hours after we landed in Melbourne a storm started to blow in. The wind was tossing tons of sand off the ocean floor and onto the coast. Roy told me that it was after such winds that he had made many of his finds of Spanish coins. I was anxious to get out with a metal detector myself.

When we went out, the wind had slowed, but it was still blowing and the waves were lashing the beach with a vengeance. It wasn't possible to keep dry, so I was glad we had brought along warm windbreakers.

We put on our earphones, tuned our machines, and went to work. It was the first of five beaches that we would work in the next week. In that time we would find thirteen Spanish coins and a Spanish medallion.

I've always appreciated the value of earphones, but never so much as I did that day. The wind was cold and the waves thundered in on the beach.

It seemed logical to me that if there were coins being thrown out of the water they would be near the water's edge, and that's where I worked. Roy, however, kept above the high-water mark.

Once I had found my first coin—a Spanish two real—and Roy still had not found any, I was more convinced than ever. The coin was coral-encrusted and hardly recognizable, but it was my first Spanish coin. I was out of my head with excitement.

I started working that beach as if there were no tomorrow, swinging the detector head back and forth as if looking for a manhole cover. Roy slowed me down, and as soon as he did, I found a copper Spanish religious medallion.

Going slow when I wanted to rush was really painful, but I watched Roy who kept working in his methodical way. I did my best to follow his example. Slow is the surest, he had told me. It was an hour before I found anything else. This was a Spanish four real, on which there was a partial date — "14." Often the Spanish did not stamp the full date on a coin. In this case it had to be a 1714 coin.

Once or twice Roy came down to the water's edge, but then he would return above the high-water mark. He wasn't finding anything there, and it seemed strange to me that he kept looking. But then he was the professional and I was the fortunate amateur who had just found two of the most valuable coins in the world — I mean to me.

The next morning we moved to a different beach. The wind was still blowing, and the wind-whipped waves lashing at the shore at high tide kept us both above the high-water mark.

It seemed to me that the day was going to be a waste. Roy hadn't found anything the day before, and the three items I had uncovered had been at the water's edge.

Because of that I wasn't too enthusiastic as I worked. I found myself thinking more about what was out there in the ocean than about any hard-core land searching. I was listening to my signal, but I admit that I was doing it without a great deal of concentration. Roy, on the other hand, was doing what he had done the previous day — slowly and methodically — and finding nothing.

An hour passed and I turned off my machine and sat on the bluff looking out at the water. It didn't seem to be any calmer. Every once in a while I'd catch sight of Roy and wonder how he could work the way he did without taking a break. I saw him drop to his knees and start digging with his hands, but I didn't pay much attention. Both of us had found a half-dozen or so tear tabs from soda pop cans and I guessed that he was picking up another. Then he started waving for me to join him.

In his hand was an irregular-shaped light green coin, much larger than those I had found. The coin was coral-encrusted, but part of the Spanish shield could be seen. Without Roy telling me, I knew it was a piece-of-eight. It was similar to one he had given me as a Christmas gift.

It didn't look like much, but Roy assured me that it would clean up beautifully. It did, but how beautifully we didn't know until we reached home and soaked it in muriatic acid. It was a full-date 1714 coin. This type sells for about $250.

● ● ●

My find restored Dick's enthusiasm immediately, and I had to laugh to myself as I watched him. He was staring at the ground as he listened to his detector signal as if trying to see through the sand. However, after a time and several more tear tabs, he drifted back toward the water's edge again. The tide by then had receded. As soon as he did, he found another two-real coin.

It was his fourth find, and it made me start second-guessing myself. I began to think that perhaps I should be working closer to the water as well. However, in the past I had made some of my best finds above the high-water mark. I kept searching there.

We had brought sandwiches and orangeade with us and we stopped for lunch. We were alone on the beach; the weather was still nasty, but neither of us cared. Dick had located his first Spanish coins and I knew I had one good enough to pay for the trip.

After eating, we returned to the search. It felt great to be alive. I love the sea, the clean smell of it, and as I moved along my mind was wandering to the things I had done and the things that Dick and I were going to do.

Then it happened. The signal in my ears was so loud that I thought I had found a beach buggy. Because of that I really didn't think of a coin. I dug slowly. It could have been something sharp and I didn't want a cut finger. Then there it was.

I had seen Spanish eight-escudo Golden Royals before—a 1714, a 1713, and two 1702s. But no one thought a 1715 existed. Comparatively few 1715 gold coins had been taken from the wrecks.

I picked it up and held it in my hands—both hands, but they were trembling so much that I had to rest them on the sand. I knew I had found the super coin of all the Spanish specie ever minted. Kneeling there with my hands on the ground, I started shouting.

• • •

With the wind and with my earphones on, I didn't hear Roy. I saw him kneeling on the sand in kind of a funny position. I kept on detecting until he started to wave with one hand. At first I thought he was ill and needed help.

When I ran up to him, he was still kneeling with the coin in his cupped palms and his hands planted firmly on the sand as if they were growing there.

I knelt next to him. Never had I seen anything like it, but I had no idea of the magnitude of the find. "Is it worth much?" I asked.

Roy grinned. Then I think he giggled. I don't remember, because the words started pouring out of his mouth faster than I had ever heard him speak before. What I gathered from everything he said was that perhaps no other single coin found by one person was as valuable. Perhaps it wasn't his words but his actions that told me that. When I reached for the coin, his eyes popped and he shouted, "Don't!"

I didn't. Then he handed it to me. "Don't drop it," he pleaded.

Since we both had our hands on the ground, I didn't know where he expected me to drop it to, but I promised him that I wouldn't.

It was heavy, and strangely warm. Then I realized why. Roy was perspiring. He had warmed it with his hands.

For the next thirty minutes we sat admiring and discussing the coin; then Roy carefully wrapped it in his handkerchief and put it in his pocket. It was getting late, yet we were reluctant to leave. The area might have been a hot spot. But we were to find nothing else there.

On the long walk back to the truck we had borrowed, the wind seemed to pick up and it cut through our clothing. We didn't mind. We had, after all, found gold in the wake of a storm.

2
Treasure Under Your Feet

Not everyone is going to make a spectacular find such as Roy did, but the point is that there *are* discoveries to be made, and most of the treasure is under your feet. Conservatively, it has been estimated that two percent of all coins ever minted have been lost. The purpose of this book is to help you find those coins as well as other kinds of treasure.

We will explain the differences in metal detectors, how to select the best one for you, and the tricks in properly tuning them. Then, most importantly, we will tell you where to search, and how to clean, care for, and dispose of your finds.

Our guest writers will take you into ghost towns, allow you to travel over Civil War and World War II battlefields, to the sites of life-and-death dramas between Indians and white invaders, and will relate how a find on land launched one of the best-equipped treasure-hunting corporations in the United States.

One of the most important coin auctioneers in the world will detail the potential of certain finds.

You will discover that all treasure does not glitter.

Another of our experts has developed a unique way of coin-shooting in lakes and ponds. The old swimming hole is like the old ball park regarding coins and rings. Every time someone takes something away, someone else makes a fresh deposit.

We will also share some of our own experiences with you. One of the most intriguing is the treasure of the river wreck, which, as we consider it, was probably what led us to write this book.

11

This volume is a handbook. It is intended as an aid. It is not just for those who think they have a clue to a golden cache. The clues will be supplied, and it won't be necessary for anyone to leave their home towns unless they wish. The treasure to be discussed is very real. Only you can't see it yet.

I'll let Roy introduce our first guest writer, coin auctioneer Hans M. F. Schulman.

• • •

(Photo supplied by Hans M. F. Schulman)

Hans M. F. Schulman.

I knew about Hans long before I met him. When we finally did meet, it was to discuss the 1715 Golden Royal. But I was aware of much of his past even before then.

Hans, who was born in Amsterdam, is descended from a long line of numismatists. He studied at the University of Amsterdam and at the Sorbonne in Paris.

He opened his offices in New York City in 1939 and has since conducted many major auctions. Over the course of his long career, he has had numerous famous clients, among them King Farouk of Egypt, former King Umberto II of Italy, and actor Adolphe Menjou.

In November 1965, he made numismatic headlines when he sold at auction the extremely rare 1825 silver rouble of the Russian Grand Duke Konstantine Pavlovich for $41,000, then the record realization for any coin.

Several years ago Hans was called on by the United States government to appraise the foreign gold coins in the magnificent Josiah Lilly Collection. The collection, valued at well over $5,000,000, was contributed to the Smithsonian Institution in Washington, D.C.

In 1951 he was appointed by President Truman to the United States Assay Commission, the first time a professional coin dealer received that honor. In that position he organized the exhibit of the United States Treasury at the First International Numismatic Exhibition in Madrid the same year.

For many years Hans was the vice-president of the International Association of Professional Numismatists, which he helped found in 1950. He holds a life membership in the American Numismatic Association, along with memberships in many other numismatic organizations in the United States and abroad.

3
The Realm of the Coin
by Hans M. F. Schulman

Countless numbers of ancient and classic coins are in collectors' hands today because of some fortunate accident or through the efforts of diligent archeologists or treasure hunters.

Significant finds have been made in sunken treasure ships as well as in underground and above-ground hiding places. In fact, wresting coins from the ocean floors has brought a tremendous amount of drama into numismatics in the last decade or so.

Most hoards, however, are discovered underground or in secret places at ground level—these are the so-called *dry treasures*. Coins recovered from shipwrecks are known as *wet treasures*.

Farmers on occasion come across treasure troves while plowing their fields. Other unexpected finds have been made by construction and demolition workers.

For example, a fourteen-year-old farmboy plowing a field with a tractor at Sussex, England, in 1959 uncovered more than 500 copper, silver, and gold coins (circa 1650). The boy's parents contacted the Sussex Archeological Society. The curator immediately went to the site and discovered several hundred more silver and copper coins in a large jar. From the way the cache was found, the curator surmised that the coins were probably a life savings hurriedly buried for safekeeping.

According to English treasure-trove law, those coins not required for the local museum—in this case the Sussex Archeological Society's museum—or the British Museum in London, can be retained by the finder. The Sussex museum retained most of the hoard for its own display and rewarded the boy with a sum equal to the full market value of the coins. Later, a number of the rarer pieces were turned over to the British Museum's collection.

Tens of thousands of items have been added to the British Museum's enormous numismatic collection through the treasure-trove laws.

In the summer of 1960, a Roman urn filled with several thousand coins was discovered in Gloucester, England, and was enthusiastically described by the leading numismatic publications as a "very important find."

The urn, measuring twelve inches by sixteen inches, was found by workmen digging in a basement. The coins were promptly turned over to the Gloucester City Museum. Most of the coins, which included silver, bronze, and a few gold pieces, were minted in the third century A.D. during the Roman occupation of Britain. The coins bore the portraits of Roman emperors Aurelian, Tacitus, Probus, and Carinus.

Many of these coins were not required either by the Gloucester City Museum or by the British Museum, and thus they eventually found their way into the hands of private collectors.

Since civilization in Britain has flourished for more than 2,000 years, old coins are frequently found. In Britain, objects of gold or silver (including coins, plate, and bullion) that have been hidden in the soil or in buildings, and to which the original owner cannot be traced, are treasure trove, and by law the property of the Crown.

This law is strictly enforced, since gold and silver coins often have great importance for historical and archeological reasons. A finder who fails to report may be guilty of a criminal offense. As we've indicated, however, the finder is compensated at full market value for all coins retained by the British museums.

Whenever a fresh hoard is unearthed, an air of high excitement sweeps through the numismatic world. Sometimes coins thought to be rare become common, prices fluctuate wildly, and often specific phases of numismatic history must be rewritten.

A prime example would be the Alexander the Great silver tetradrachm with its head of Herakles and the seated figure of Zeus with his eagle and thunderbolt. This was one of the most widely

(Dick Richmond Photos)

The front and back sides of a Roman coin found in England.

circulated coins of ancient times, but for years prices for these specimens in choice condition were relatively high.

This finely wrought and highly artistic tetradrachm circulated all through Alexander's empire and continued to be issued by his successors for almost 200 years after his death in 323 B.C. These coins eventually replaced the issues of the individual Greek city-states.

Interestingly enough, during the last century many hoards of the tetradrachms have turned up. One of the largest was unearthed at Damanhur in Egypt in 1905 — more than 8,000 tetradrachms, buried about 318 B.C. were brought to light. Consequently, prices dropped sharply and collectors of even modest means were able to add this beautiful coin to their cabinets.

During the course of the Roman and Greek civilizations, people of wealth collected coins. The Greeks collected issues of the myraid of city-states, while the wealthy Romans collected both Greek coins and the various provincial issues of the Roman Empire. When these ancient collections are found today, the numismatic world is, indeed, greatly enriched.

Countless persons who lived during Europe's medieval period — people who were both wealthy and not so wealthy — buried their money for safekeeping. A person would ordinarily hide his money somewhere around his house, especially if he were departing on a trip.

If the person did not return, the coins were simply lost — sometimes for hundreds of years. A farmer in the province of Zealand in the Netherlands while working in his garden a few years ago stumbled on a king's ransom of gold coins dated from the late 1500s to the mid-1640s.

Called the Serooskerke Find, consisting primarily of coins struck for circulation throughout the Netherlands, the coins became the topic of television, radio, and newspaper reports throughout the world.

My cousin, Jacques, who heads the House of Schulman in Amsterdam (a numismatic firm that has been in operation since 1880), conducted a public auction of the Serooskerke Find treasures in November 1966.

The auction attracted bidders from around the world. Record prices were realized for many of the coins. A gold ducat of King William IV (1546–86) drew a winning bid of $1,500. A 1586 gold rose noble struck for the town of Gorinchem realized the same amount.

The Serooskerke Find auction catalogue is today considered a classic publication in the field of numismatic literature. Coins hitherto unknown were brought to light and catalogued for the first time.

A collector's life is not always a smooth one. A celebrated European collector who had located a cache of Roman gold and silver coins not far from Knidos in Turkey suffered a misadventure. As he was admiring the treasure on the plane from Smyrna to Istanbul, he found he was being watched. As he stepped from the plane, he was arrested by Turkish police. According to the country's treasure-trove laws, treasures found in Turkey stay in Turkey. The collector was lucky he wasn't thrown in jail.

Significant numismatic hoards have been found in Russia within recent years, and these finds, too, must not be taken out of the country. Woe to the numismatist or archeologist who tries to put one over on the Soviet government.

Over a period of years, the Schulman Coin and Mint has conducted numerous auction sales that have featured both *dry treasure* and *wet treasure* coins. Among the dry treasures, for example; we've handled some of the noted gold Aboukir medals, which were struck by the Greeks for the Olympic Games held in honor of Alexander the Great during the Hellenistic Age in 242-43 A.D.

These fabulous medals were discovered in 1905 by a group of poor Arabs who stumbled across them in the dry sands of the desert near Aboukir Bay at the Rosetta mouth area of the Nile River in Egypt. Whenever the Aboukir gold medals are sold at public auction, they gain wide attention in the numismatic press.

Among the wet treasure sales we've conducted, probably the most important was the Spanish Galleon Treasure auction at the Waldorf Astoria Hotel in November 1972. Perhaps we might relate the essential elements of the dramatic background of this sale in the brief space we've been allotted here.

Early in 1715 a group of eleven Spanish ships called at ports throughout the Spanish Empire in Latin America. There they filled their chests with coins and ingots of silver and gold, together with a plethora of other valuable artifacts that were produced at such cities as Cuzco and Lima in Peru, Santa Fe de Bogota in Colombia, and Mexico City. All these cities maintained highly productive mints under the supervision of Spain.

Once loaded the eleven ships rendezvoused at Havana, Cuba. In July, a fleet was formed under the joint command of Captain General Juan Esteban de Ubilla and Don Antonio de Echeverz. On July 27, the ships weighed anchor and set sail for Spain, following a northeasterly course. Since the Spanish captain wanted to stay in sight of land for as long as possible, the fleet hugged the coast of Florida.

Then on the fateful night of July 30-31, the sky darkened to an eerie blue-black, the wind rose, and the fleet found itself in the midst of an awesome hurricane. Ten of the eleven ships were literally pounded to death on the jagged reefs, some losing all hands.

Both Ubilla and Echeverz were lost in the storm. Only the *Grifon*, a French ship commanded by Captain Don Antonio Dare and sailing under the Spanish flag, managed to survive by staying clear of the reefs. Ironically enough, Dare got through the catastrophe by disobeying fleet orders and sailing one-half point farther northeast.

Along with the ten ships, more than 1,000 men were lost in the hurricane, together with at least $15,000,000 in registered treasure. Historians record this as one of the great sea disasters.

Within a year the Spanish government dispatched a salvage team to recover the treasure. It seems that less than half was saved. The other half had to wait 250 years until Kip Wagner, an American and the founder of the Real Eight Company, came along to complete the job, or complete it insofar as it was humanly possible to do so — a scattering of coins and artifacts still remain in the briny deep covered by tons of sand.[1]

In discovering the exact location of the wrecked Spanish fleet and salvaging its treasure, Wagner (who died at the age of 65 on February 26, 1972) unquestionably scored the greatest single numismatic achievement of the twentieth century. Through his determined efforts, literally thousands of coins once thought to be irretrievably lost are now being pumped into the mainstream of the numismatic world.

Kip Wagner really is the embodiment of the American dream. A native of Miamisburg, Ohio, he first visited Florida in 1921 as a boy of fifteen. During the 1920s and 1930s, Wagner developed a successful contracting business in Ohio. After World War II he moved to his favorite spot, the Wabasso-Sebastian area in Florida.

Continuing his contracting work in Florida, he built motels and other structures; his specialty was masonry and plastering. One day in the mid-1950s while walking along the beach near Cape Canaveral, Wagner spotted an irregularly shaped piece of silver on which was stamped a cross and the arms of Spain. This was, of course, a real eight-cob coin.

This accidental find did something to Wagner; his curiosity was aroused because he strongly felt there must be other coins lying out somewhere in the ocean waiting to be picked up. Soon he invested fifteen dollars in an army surplus mine detector, and from that point on, he was an authentic treasure hunter.

In 1959 Wagner brought together a small group of kindred spirits to form the nucleus of the Real Eight Company. At first the treasure hunters had little luck. Occasionally they did find some cob silver

1. See Chapter 21.

The 1714 eight-escudo Spanish Golden Royal.

pieces, a few cannon balls, and other small relics, but nothing of real significance. Their efforts seemed to be hit and miss until Kip realized that none of the coins he found were dated after 1715.

This was the clue that led him directly to the big strike. With the help of Dr. Kip Kelso, a Sebastian physician, Wagner obtained some 3,000 feet of microfilm manuscripts from the Archives of the Indies in Seville, Spain.

After the two men succeeded in translating the documents, they pieced together the story of the wrecked Spanish plate fleet. With an amazing degree of accuracy, they determined the resting places of the wrecked ships from Sebastian Inlet south to Fort Pierce. The treasure hunters took up their work once more.

For a couple of years, the townspeople of Fort Pierce had laughed at these men who went to sea every day in a specially equipped ship and who came back at night virtually empty-handed. Then, one day, Wagner and company returned with more than 1,000 gold coins, worth at least $1,000,000; the laughing ceased.

During the 1960s Real Eight salvaged perhaps $5,000,000 in treasure. The boom came between 1964 and 1967. We should also point out that according to Florida law, Real Eight had to turn over twenty-five percent of all their treasure finds to the state. This regulation was scrupulously followed by Real Eight.

Florida has never sold its share of the treasure, choosing instead to place all its specimens in museums throughout the state.

Various sections of the Real Eight treasure were sold at public

The 1715 eight-escudo Spanish Golden Royal.

auction as early as October 1964. It was in our November 1972 sale, however, that we offered the heart of the collection. Under the hammer we placed approximately 1,000 gold coins, 2,000 silver ones, and dozens of artifacts.

These coins are extremely important in furthering numismatic scholarship. Fully eighty percent of the specimens salvaged by Real Eight were previously unknown in the numismatic world, and, as a consequence, standard reference works are now being revised.

Water, of course, does not affect gold, with the result that the gold pieces usually appear as if they had just come out of the presses of the Latin American mints.

The prize coins in the November 1972 sale were the eight-escudo Royals dated 1702 and 1714. The Royals were those coins specially designed and struck for King Philip V of Spain. The eight-escudo Royals brought winning bids in the $20,000 range, but they certainly would be worth far more today. The sale also included other Royals, among them several four-escudo denominations.

We are now able to report that a 1715 eight-escudo Golden Royal struck at the Mexico City mint for Philip V has been found along the beaches of east Florida by Roy Volker. The coin is undoubtedly a part of the treasure cargo of the 1715 plate fleet. Technically, however, the coin is probably dry treasure rather than wet since it was found on land rather than in water. The waves simply washed the coin up on the shore.[2]

According to all evidence we have, the 1715 Golden Royal is a

2. See Chapter 1.

unique coin, the only one of its kind that has ever been found. Since the last of the ships in the fleet were loaded in July of that year, most of the coins on board were dated, logically enough, no later than 1714. In fact, the dates on the coins range from the early 1690s to 1714.

Dr. Leopold Lopez-Chavez, in his authoritative catalogue of Spanish World coins, *La Onza de a Ocho*, shows a photo of the 1714 eight-escudo Royal (under No. 287), but for the 1715 date eight-escudo Royal (under No. 288) he lists only the crude "regular" type cob. He makes no mention of the possible existence of any 1715 Royals.

The 1714 Royal as illustrated in Dr. Lopez-Chavez's catalogue, as well as in our own 1972 Treasure Sale catalogue, is quite different from the 1715 specimen. On the 1715 coin, instead of three small lilies in the center of the Bourbon shield, the three lilies are very large and fill up the shield's entire center. On the 1715, the crown is less ornate than on the 1714, and there are other differences in design.

We would estimate the value of the 1715 eight-escudo Golden Royal to be at least in the $50,000 to $75,000 price range. While a coin of this magnificence and historic value would crown the most distinguished private collection, it really would be more appropriately placed in one of the great Spanish museums.

Actually, this is a very conservative valuation for a historic and unique specimen; a number of rare coins have already been sold for $100,000 or more recently, including the United States 1804 Silver Dollar and the 1913 Liberty Nickel.

Treasure hunting challenges the imagination of numismatists more than ever. We might also point out that sophisticated metal detecting equipment and new types of scientific instruments have made the job of treasure hunting a bit easier. In fact, the whole business of seeking treasure has become a great deal more organized.

We might only emphasize that it requires a considerable amount of fortitude, planning, hard work, and patience to become a truly successful treasure hunter. And if the modern-day treasure hunter wants someone to emulate, he can do no better than to study the methods of the late Kip Wagner.

4
Differences in Metal Detectors

Now that Hans has told you that the treasure is out there, perhaps Dick and I can help you get some of it. The first step is knowing that there are differences in metal detectors, and you should have some idea of what those differences are.

Trial and error is one way to an education, and sometimes it is the only way. However, it can be time-consuming and expensive. By explaining the variations in machines, we can help you select the best one for your purposes and at the same time save you time and money.

Most detectors presently on the market are either transmitter-receivers (TRs) or beat frequency operated (BFOs). The electronic circuitry in each is different and, consequently, so is the signal that each emits.

The TR system sends out a constant tone that increases in loudness when passed over metal. The BFO models have a gargling sound emitted by a steady beat that increases in speed near metal.

I have found that the TR has greater sensitivity and therefore greater penetration. Then, too, in my experience the TR has been more accurate in pinpointing.

The most important thing in using a metal detector correctly is learning how to fine-tune your instrument.[1] It is difficult to fine-tune an instrument that has a signal that drifts. While the TRs do drift to a small degree, the drift is considerably less than in the BFO system.

Besides the TR and the BFOs there are other systems on the

1. See Chapter 6.

market such as the differential detectors, the low-frequency types, and the pulse induction units.

The differential detectors are designed to recognize and reject metallic paper, pull-tabs from cans, and bottle caps, all of which sound like coins. Until recently this only sounded like the treasure hunter's best friend. Most of those developed worked to a degree, but none of them had as much zip as the TR.

But one of the largest manufacturers of metal detectors in the world has just made a couple of breakthroughs, and the differential detector, which the company calls the TR discriminator, is one of them.

Instead of Low-High-Auto modes, the discriminator has Normal-Auto-Discriminate modes and a separate control for adjusting the degree of discrimination. Simply, this means that the Discriminate control can be used to filter out metallic paper and all the other annoying items that most of us dig up in our search for coins. What happens is that the signal cuts out when it passes over junk.

It's not a miracle machine—wonderful is good enough—but the control can be adjusted so that an upside-down bottle cap is rejected at the same time as it clearly detects a nickel. Pull tabs will not be rejected by this instrument, but the signal will be weak by comparison.

If that isn't good enough, the discriminator can be adjusted to reject the tear tabs, too, and still detect most coins. *Most* coins.

To my way of thinking, that only leaves one serious flaw in the differential models. They are designed to reject ferrous material. Hoards of coins are known to have been hidden in iron boxes. And sometimes the searcher discovers his riches by finding trash first, especially bottle collectors who scratch for dumps to uncover their prizes.

The depth penetration on the new discriminator is satisfactory, but on most other models it is usually several inches less than either the TRs or the BFOs. Two or three inches more penetration can be the difference between finding a relatively new coin and a valuable old one.

Some of the best metal detectors ever produced are the low-

Roy Volker (left) and Dick Richmond with a spread of some of the coins and rings and other objects they found.
(Don Paule Photo)

frequency models. These are the granddaddies. They were developed for the armed forces during World War II as mine detectors. And, as Hans mentioned, it was with that kind of unit that Kip Wagner launched his quest that brought him millions. That's for those who think there's no romance in discussing metal detectors.

But back to the explanation. Since World War II, manufacturers have refined the low-frequency models so that they are better than ever. They are very sensitive and are especially effective on beaches, where salt water and mineralization have little effect on them.[2]

They are, however, also heavy, and in more ways than one. A full day's work with one of these armed forces units can cause some real

2. See Chapter 9.

muscle aches. But the heaviest part is price. It costs the government about $2,000 apiece for these units, which has put them out of the range of most buyers. Until now.

I mentioned above that a manufacturer has made a couple of breakthroughs. The second one is a machine that the firm calls a ground exclusion balance unit, which means a super low-cost (relatively), low-frequency, lightweight metal detector. I spent months testing it myself, and I believe that it is the biggest contribution in the field in the last thirty years.

There is a control on it called a Terranean Attenuator, which minimizes effects of loop height variations caused by mineralized ground. It does not respond to black magnetic sand or mineralized ground that usually interferes with the detection of coins, rings, and other metal objects. In effect, I found that the instrument achieves ultrasensitivity for exceptional depth detection regardless of soil conditions.

With it, I have gone over areas that had been searched with other detectors and found old coins that had previously been too deep to be detected. Then, too, I have been able to search areas that in the past used to drive me crazy because of the mineralized conditions of the soil.

Until recently I favored the TR model. I still use it most of the time, and I am well aware that the vast numbers of metal detectors in use and on the market are the transmitter-receiver types. But the unit is only as good as its operator. The TR transmits an electromagnetic signal. When the signal hits a metal object, the sound changes. If the coin is deep, the signal will be faint. Proper tuning is, of course, essential.[3]

To insure proper reception requires a set of good earphones. Unfortunately, only a few manufacturers furnish a good set with their units. The importance of earphones cannot be overemphasized. They keep external noises such as cars, trucks, and airplanes to a minimum. Even away from an urban area, there are noises that interfere with productive detecting. Birds, the wind whistling through trees, and the ocean rolling in on a beach can inspire a poet; to the treasure hunter, they can be extremely distracting—sometimes without his even being aware of it.

3. See Chapter 6.

Often the greatest distractions are curious children. Metal detecting seems to draw them like a magnet. Earphones can save you from endless questions by simply pointing to them and saying you cannot hear what is being asked.

Most importantly, earphones enable the hunter to detect the faint sounds that usually are the signal of something deep. The deeper the finds, the older the objects. And old coins are more valuable than new ones.

There are meters on the more expensive metal detectors. Usually they have two functions. One is a battery check, and the other gives the operator a visual readout of the signal. Few treasure hunters pay much attention to the meter as a practical tool. It is too difficult to search in any kind of pattern while watching a needle bounce around. In most cases, a coin can be heard before it can be seen on a meter.

The average detector in the $100 to $200 price range usually comes with a six-inch to eight-inch diameter loop (coil). This loop can be used to detect shallow-buried coins or larger objects as deep as two to three feet down.

Unless you have a specific project in mind, this loop will suffice for all your detecting needs — at least at first. The deluxe models freqently have two loops; one six to eight inches in diameter, and the other ten to eleven inches in diameter.

The six to eight-inch loops produce a concentrated magnetic field that will pinpoint an object as small as a one-cent piece six to seven inches deep. The magnetic field of the larger loop is not as concentrated. It works beautifully for larger objects, but is not satisfactory for pinpointing coins. Thus, there is seldom a use for a larger loop if you are coinshooting.

Waterproof loops come with all deluxe instruments. In an inexpensive unit, you will probably have to pay an additional charge to get one. It is worth the price. Loops that are not waterproofed often have condensation problems after working in wet grass. Then, too, you never know when you may want to submerge the head along some beach.

5
Selecting a Metal Detector

Laying out money for a metal detector can be like blowing $20 for a left-handed screwdriver with a wobble socket. Or it can be an investment in fun and profit.

The prices of the instruments range from $19.95 to $2,000. Units that sell for less than $100 are little more than toys. Those in the $100 to $200 price range are the most popular with first-time buyers. And, in fact, they probably fit the needs of most coin-shooters. Above $200 are detectors for the hard-core hobbyists, which is what most of us become once we start finding things.

There are so many manufacturers — which is the right one? This is the question most of us ask whenever we buy anything these days. Every manufacturer advertises his product as being the best. How do you know?

One good way is to ask a friend who is already addicted. If none of your friends fall into that category, check the Yellow Pages of your telephone directory. You will probably find a dealer under Metal Locating Equipment.

Visit the dealer and ask for a demonstration. Check the features of one brand against the other, then decide.

If you live in a small town or a rural area where there are no dealers, write to several of the larger manufacturers. If a company does not have a dealer within 100 miles of where you live, find one that does.

Your best bet is to buy from a dealer who can show you how to use the unit properly, as well as supplying you with tips that will save you many hours of trial and error and frustration.

Many dealers rent units. Renting a unit before a first purchase is an ideal approach. You get an opportunity to try your hand at metal detecting and to test the quality of the equipment you might purchase. Dealers who rent units often deduct the rental price from the purchase price should you decide to buy.

Every manufacturer has literature describing its product, and most of what is written is honest. However, there is nothing better than testing a unit yourself.

As a last-resort source of supply, there are mail-order-only companies. Most of these operate from post office boxes and answering services. They have no dealers; if the unit you purchase malfunctions, you may have difficulty getting it replaced or repaired. Knowing that, if you still want to gamble, remember that it is a gamble.

A few manufacturers have repair stations scattered throughout the United States. When you purchase your unit, find out where the closest repair station is. Save the box in which your unit came so you have something in which to pack it should you ever have to return it for adjustment. It is a good idea to insure the instrument and ask for a signed return receipt.

There are some manufacturers who supply metal detectors in kit form. If you like to know what makes an instrument tick, hum, or gargle, the kits might interest you. However, the do-it-yourself models never seem to function as well as the factory-assembled units.

6
Tuning Your Detector

Everyone who owns a television set knows what a difference fine tuning can make. With television a person can see the changes, but fine-tuning a metal detector is a little harder.

Yet its importance cannot be overemphasized. It will make the difference between finding a little or a lot.

The beat-frequency unit is tuned by holding the sensing head (loop) about an inch above the ground so that you obtain the minimum number of beats per second. As you pass the sensing head over metal, you will hear the beat increase.

The transmitter-receiver unit can be tuned to its greatest sensitivity very simply. Lay the sensing head on the ground. Put no pressure on it. Then turn the detector on and turn the tuning knob until you can hear a faint yet steady hum.

Earphones will help in this respect, enabling you to reduce your volume control to almost nothing. The purpose of this is that it increases the sensitivity of your fine-tuning control. Now you will listen for not only abrupt changes in the hum but also faint changes in the hum. A faint change indicates something deep, and that is where the older and more valuable coins are. This is not a magic formula. It simply takes practice, but it does work.

Your detector will do the job for you if you know how to get the most out of it.

Often you can tune your detector and work with it for some time before you have to retune it. Yet why take a chance on missing something valuable? Retuning as you work soon becomes natural.

Hillsides are a small problem because you have to retune as you change elevations, but it is not difficult and it will come to you with practice.

7
Practice Shooting

Hours of practice are not necessary before the real hunt begins, but even professional golfers use putting greens to get the feel of things. What I'm suggesting is that a little prepared coinshooting can be just as valuable to you.

Bury coins of the same size at different depths and coins of varying sizes at the same depths, then listen to the strength of the sound each gives you. See how deeply you can bury a coin and still detect it.

When you think you have that perfected, bury a bottle cap and a pull tab from a can to see if you can tell the difference between those irritating items and coins. The sounds each gives off is unique; in time you will be able to know the difference. It's like learning a foreign language; it's baffling at first, then suddenly you have it and the strain is over.

You'll notice that the coins you buried deeply will give off a faint sound, making them difficult to locate. They can be found only if you work slowly.

Those buried close to the surface can be located easily even when quickly sweeping over the ground with your sensing head. The pace at which you sweep will determine how many old coins you'll dig up.

Being fine-tuned is the first important step in detecting, but you must allow your sensing head (and your ears) time to pick up deeper objects. So slow down and find more.

Successful treasure hunting is systematic, whether it is on a large scale or is just funtime coinshooting. Work an area one section at a time, keeping track of the ground covered so you won't go over it again.

The normal sweep of the sensing head should never be more than four feet. If you walk backwards you will find it easier to stay in a pattern.

8
Recovery of Coins and Care of Lawns

The thoughtlessness of a few has caused some cities to close public parks to metal detector users. Not enough can be said about leaving an area with no visible holes or other signs of damage.

Of the many considerations you should make before coinshooting, selecting a proper metal detector to pinpoint small finds and learning how to use it before searching on public property have already been discussed. Another item for careful consideration is the selection of a proper digging tool.

Most detector users have several tools to cover different situations. For well-manicured lawns, where cutting a plug and replacing it might be objectionable, a six-inch to eight-inch screwdriver is functional. However, a plastic probe such as the tip end of a fishing rod, also six to eight inches long, inserted into the handle of an ice pick is probably better. This type of tool will not scratch or damage a good coin.

A stout six-inch hunting knife is another practical tool. Once the coin is pinpointed, a small plug can be cut, removed, and later replaced. In areas such as Arizona where grass is difficult to grow, plugs should not be cut. Plugs completely separated from the rest of the lawn will die.

Instead of cutting out a plug, a half-circle should be cut and the grass folded back. Once the find has been removed, the soil is replaced and the grass put back. With this method, there will be no evidence that a coin was ever removed.

In areas where the grass is thick, a small but sturdy garden trowel is a must. Using the point of the trowel, a plug can be cut out of the grass. Before digging further, check the plug to see if the find is inside. If it is not, dig the find, then replace the soil and the plug.

9
Soft Ground and Mineralization

Dick and I have found that the season often determines the most productive time for coinshooting—specifically, when the ground is soft and moist. In the Midwest that includes spring, autumn, and the warmer winter days. In summer, the ground is usually hard and dry, except after showers, and treasure hunting is therefore unproductive. When the ground is moist, metal detectors are more sensitive. Often the penetration is greater by thirty-five to forty percent.

I once worked a park in a small town, concentrating in the area around the bandstand. The park was old but not covered with pull tabs and bottle caps. It looked like a good place to search. But all I found were two V nickels and one Indian head penny. Not one new coin, which led me to suspect that someone else had covered the ground before.

It was summer and the ground was baked hard. With such small finds for my trouble, I normally wouldn't have returned.

Chance brought me back about six months later when the ground was soft and moist. I was passing through town and stopped for a sandwich at a cafe across the street from the park. Finishing my sandwich, I decided to recheck the park just for the heck of it.

I turned my unit on and a minute or two later found the first of several barber dimes that I walked away with that day.

It was morning when I started and evening when I finished. In that time, I concentrated my efforts in an area no larger than fifty feet square. I found almost a hundred coins, and most, maybe eighty percent, were from 1880 to 1930.

36

The coins had been there during my first visit, but the soft damp ground simply aided me the second time around.

Like moisture, or the lack of it, mineralization can cause your detector to perform differently in every area you work. One park just a few city blocks from another can be harder to work because mineralization makes it more difficult to tune your instrument.

There is no mistaking an area in which mineralization is high because of the background noise. The differences in detection between areas of low and high mineralization can be as much as eight inches in depth for the same machine on the same size coin.

In the West it is often possible to detect a dime at ten to twelve inches in an area of low mineralization. Conversely, along the seashore a person can detect background noise where the sand is wet. It is not the moisture that causes the background noise but the minerals in the ocean water that have been impregnated in the sand.

Where the moisture works for you as a conductor in areas of low mineralization, it works against you here. It is still a conductor, but it is conducting everything. And, hence, the noise.

A saltwater beach is a perfect example to use to explain what we mean about problems with mineralization. Near the water, the noise makes it difficult to detect effectively. However, away from the water's edge, where the same sand with about the same mineralization is dry, the background noise disappears and your machine will allow you to hear things at greater depths.

Most manufacturers claim their machines can be retuned under these circumstances to eliminate the noise caused by the high mineral saturation. What they are actually saying is that you can detune your machine to eliminate the noise. When you detune, you lose the normal sensitivity and depth of which your detector is capable.

That is a real limitation of a high-frequency detector, and there is not much that can be done about it. However, it is fair to say that on those parts of the beach where the sand is consistently wet the sand is also packed, which means that a coin or any other object disappearing beneath the surface is more than likely not too deep.

Many people living near the ocean use low-frequency metal detectors but these can be a problem too.[1]

1. See Chapter 4.

10
Coinshooting Is Thirsty Work

Ever wonder why soldiers are taught to dig foxholes? It seems the most natural thing in the world. If someone is shooting at him, a man would naturally want to burrow into the earth. Apparently the army has determined that the men who know how to burrow ahead of time have a better chance of survival.

Well, Roy and I will extend that philosophy and bend it a little so that it can be applied to metal detecting.

When most people first start coinshooting, they figure that a metal detector and earphones are enough. We did, too, and found ourselves thirsty, hungry, and discouraged.

Superbuffs are ready for almost any contingency, often having two of everything. That is ideal, of course, but it is usually beyond the individual's budget. Yet having two machines is not really what we're discussing.

What we're suggesting are things such as a canteen or a thermos of water, a sandwich, and a candy bar. Getting into an area that is producing is like having a winning streak at the poker table. A person does not want to break the streak; yet if you don't think ahead, hunger and thirst might do it for you.

Also take along a magnifying glass. If you're finding some old coins, you'll want to know it. You can always come back of course, but soil conditions may never be that ideal again.

In some grassy areas chiggers can be a problem. We carry sulfur in a plastic squeeze-type container and squirt it on our ankles and calves before stepping into the bush.

A worker's apron is another good accessory. The pockets are a good place to store finds and trash as you search.

Digging tools have been discussed before.[1] This is just a reminder to select one that is not likely to break or bend with the first scoopful.

It's not our intention to reveal that we are truly screwballs. Rather, we would like to have you think of us as dedicated treasure finders. No matter, there's no hiding it. Later, when our experiences on Corrigan's Beach are related,[2] you will find out regardless. With that in mind, we hope to prepare you for our great fiasco with another little story of something that sounds strange at the outset but turned out to be a good idea.

Roy is constantly surprising me, and July 14, 1973, was no exception. It was the Saturday before we were to leave for the Bahamas, where Roy was to lead a treasure hunting expedition sponsored by *The National Enquirer*.[3] He and Don Paule, one of the divers who was to take part in the expedition with us, arrived at my home unannounced at about nine o'clock in the morning. I was working on a magazine article and had no intention of going anywhere with two guys with a power mower in the back of their car. I couldn't figure out what Roy was up to, and Don was unable to enlighten me. All I knew was that Roy was being mysterious and insistent at the same time.

Roy looked like a handyman about to mow lawns, which really bugged me because I knew that was not his idea of a super activity. I asked. He grinned. I looked at Don. Don shrugged. I relented, feeling as if I had again been sucked into something stupid.

The three of us drove into the country. Roy looked smug. Don and I were confused, but we figured we'd let him have his secret and we turned the conversation to our forthcoming trip.

At least we started to. Just as we got into it, Roy pulled the car to a stop in front of an abandoned farmhouse that still had a hint of elegance about it. We got out and, without explanation, Roy removed the mower from the trunk and began cutting the weeds on

1. See Chapter 8.
2. See Chapter 20.
3. An article on the trip appeared in the October 28, 1973 issue of *The National Enquirer*.

the east side of the building. When he had cleared a large area, he replaced the mower and took out a metal detector.

In five minutes he had his first coin, a large one-cent piece. With that, Don and I joined the search. The day did not yield a vast number of coins; there were less than forty. However, every coin except one (a new half dollar) was circa 1930 or older.

The farm had been abandoned for a number of years and Roy knew about it. Yet it wasn't until the night before the hunt that his mother happened to bring it up, telling him about the lawn parties she had attended there as a girl.

Roy remembered seeing how overgrown with weeds the place was, and he knew that detecting would be difficult unless they were cut. The mowing did not take long and the derision he suffered from Don and me on the way to the farm was repaid in full on the way back. In fact, we were still hearing about how smart he was on the expedition a week later.

11
A Metal Detector's Depth Perception

One of the most frequently asked questions that Dick and I receive regarding metal detectors concerns the depth at which one can find coins. It is a logical inquiry. The deeper the coin, the older the coin — usually. It follows that the older the coin, the more valuable it is — again, usually.

If you are to become a treasure finder, you will naturally want to uncover the best treasure available. In this chapter you will get a picture of what you can reasonably expect from your machine under normal circumstances.

Many manufacturers claim certain depths for certain sized coins with certain models. These claims are seldom underestimations.

There are other manufacturers that do not make such claims, explaining that penetration depends on a multitude of circumstances, such as mineralization, moisture in the ground,[1] and the proficiency of the operator.

That explanation is much more palatable. Then, everything else being equal, penetration will depend on the quality of the unit you are using.

Cost is not always the major factor because a $100 unit of one manufacturer may be superior to the $100 unit of another. Yet, within a single manufacturer's line, it is an indicator.

Each manufacturer usually has an economy model, a full-size and a deluxe. For convenience the instruments have been separated into three categories: A (economy), B (full-size), and C (deluxe).

The chart below shows the average penetration for a regular

1. See Chapter 9.

41

	1 cent	5 cents	10 cents	25 cents	50 cents	$1
A	3″ to 5″	3″ to 5″	3″ to 5″	4″ to 6″	5″ to 7″	6″ to 8″
B	4″ to 6″	4″ to 6″	4″ to 6″	6″ to 8″	7″ to 9″	8″ to 10″
C	6″ to 8″	6″ to 8″	6″ to 8″	7″ to 10″	8″ to 12″	12″ to 15″

one-cent piece, a nickel, a dime, a quarter, a fifty-cent piece, and a silver dollar.

Most of the coins found seem to be from two to six inches under the surface. This is an average, however, and coins are discovered much deeper.

The greatest depth at which I uncovered a coin on land was at fourteen inches. The coin was a large one-cent piece in mint condition dated 1828.

Copper coins oxidize over the years, and as they sink, they leave a trail in the soil that makes them easier to find than silver coins of the same size.

A large 1828 penny (about the size of a quarter) found by Volker. (Dick Richmond Photo)

Obviously, the larger the coin, the deeper it can be detected. there are stories of people finding silver dollars at depths from eighteen inches to two feet. This sounds like nonsense and probably is.

Under the most ideal circumstances, which would mean that the coin was lying flat in moist non-mineralized soil, would a silver dollar be found at depths greater than sixteen inches with the mass of equipment presently available?[2]

The position of the coin makes a difference as to how easily it is detected. A coin lying in the ground at an angle or on end is much harder to find than the average depth suggested in the chart.

Quite often, people have remarked to me that they believe coins rise and sink with the changes in the seasons. This is doubtful, but the psychology is based on what seems like logic. Six months after covering an area, it is possible to return to the same area and discover coins that are very old and that obviously were in the ground the first time around.[3]

The explanation for this is that the ground was in a more conducive condition regarding moisture on the second search. Thus, coins not detectable on the first pass were uncovered on the second.

Everyone would like to find really old coins, those of the nineteeth century or earlier. How deep? I have found a number of Indian head pennies just a few inches from the surface. This however, is rare.

In order to find coins consistently from around the turn of the century, a detector must have depth perception of at least six inches. The deeper the detector can "see," the earlier the coins.

An operator who knows his machine, working slowly and using earphones, will learn to dig the faint sounds; when he does that, he will consistently find coins much older than the less experienced treasure hunter.

One of the greatest mistakes a new treasure hunter makes is using his machine as if he were in a race against time. He is, in a sense. But the time is the past. And the further back the time, the harder it is to hear.

2. As I mentioned earlier, equipment is now being tested that could change that picture completely.
3. See Chapter 9.

12
Where to Search

Where there are people, there is treasure. If people have been hanging around an area for a long time, then the treasure might be old, rare, and valuable. In the United States, the eastern seaboard certainly offers potential for old and valuable finds.

Earlier in the book Dick mentioned that two percent of all coins ever minted are lying under your feet. So the best place to start detecting is right in your own backyard, especially if you happen to live in an old house.

Old Houses

If you don't live in an old house yourself, you can probably think of a dozen persons who do. Most of them more than likely would let you work their yards if you are careful to replace the plugs. Almost everyone is curious as to whether there is a cache somewhere on their property. In the back of their minds is the suspicion that someone in the past either lost or buried something of value on their real estate.

Quite frankly, the suspicion is usually correct. If a house is fifty to one hundred years old, the yard will frequently yield a multitude of coins.

Everyone has seen an old house or an estate they have admired. I'm no exception. For years I passed an old estate on my way to and from work. Like most persons, I was shy about approaching the owners to detect on their property. Yet things have a way of working out.

One day I received a call from a woman who had been referred to me by a mutual friend. The woman explained that she had been raking leaves in her backyard and had lost a diamond ring. She explained that the ring was not of great value; however, sentimentally it was very precious to her. I agreed to help.

When I arrived at the address she had given me, I discovered that her home was the very one I had been admiring all those years.

After a short conversation with the woman, I set up my search pattern. In less than fifteen minutes I found the ring.

The woman was delighted and offered to pay me for my help. I have nothing against money and normally would have accepted. But what I really wanted in this case was to use my metal detector on the rest of the property. I asked her and she agreed willingly.

Working a close pattern, and keeping my unit fine-tuned, I began finding one coin after another. It was like a money mine. When I arrived, it had been near dusk and I didn't have much time to work. In spite of that, by the time I left, my evening's collection included three Indian head pennies, an 1891 V nickel, and two barber dimes in mint condition. They were among thirty coins of the same period.

Also I discovered a silver thimble with the name of the owner's family on it. This I gave to the woman, for which I was rewarded with a standing invitation to return at any time.

I've since removed many more coins from the property. And as equipment improves, I'll return to rework this veritable piggy bank.

Old homes are good places to work because they are for the most part virgin territory. You'll be surprised at how many owners of old homes will allow you to detect on their property if you'll agree not to leave any gaping holes and offer to share anything of value that is found.

Parks

The best thing about public places is that they are reseeded with coins and other valuables regularly. Almost every large city abounds with parks. Since you want to work the oldest ones, check with the parks department and see which ones qualify.

No matter what size a park is, there are certain areas more likely to yield coins than others. One of the best places in an old park is around the bandstand. People used to lie on the grass and listen to the music. The concerts were free but they often paid a price with carelessness. This is where coins, 1800s vintage, will be found.

When working, use logic. Imagine the area around the bandstand as a pie with the bandstand in the center. More than half of that pie is going to yield very little. That is the half behind the stand. Search the large wedge in front of the stand, and listen for the deep coins, the faint sounds on your well-tuned detector.

Ball diamonds are potential winners. Start at the shortstop or second base position and work in, then reverse the process until the whole infield is covered. After that, work the sidelines.

In one instance, I was working a ball park in which I wasn't finding any surface coins, which is really unusual. Because of that I asked a groundskeeper if someone else was also detecting on the field.

I was told that every Monday an old man and his wife came out searching for coins. Knowing that, I fine-tuned my detector and worked the infield very carefully.

I dug up a handful of coins, a few medallions, and two gold rings. None of the coins were of exceptional value but the point is that this was in an area that had been worked regularly.

Picnic areas can be good and bad. They are good because of the heavy pedestrian traffic, and bad because all those pedestrians seem to be carrying cans of beer and soda pop and dropping the pull tabs for you to find. Bottle caps and pull tabs in abundance can be very frustrating, and why frustrate yourself as long as there are other places in which to search?

A fishing lake in summer is often a skating pond in winter. Both attract losers, not necessarily in life but the out-of-pocket variety. Water and the water's edge seem to have a way of luring valuables.

Money may not grow on trees, but under the limbs of the big ones you may uncover proof of Newton's law of gravity. An updated version of this is: What falls out of the pocket sometimes takes to the root. And when you're looking at trees and wondering if there is treasure below, don't ignore an old stump.

Once out of the forest, look for a large flat area near the picnic grounds. With a little imagination you can picture people running foot races, three-legged races, potato races, making all sorts of fools of themselves and paying for it at the same time.

Many parks in small towns feature annual carnivals at which Ferris wheels and other machines created to turn the stomach are erected. You may have some trouble with bottle caps here, but not as much as you may think. Chances are the concession stands have been set up some distance from the rides and the concentration of aggravation will be there.

There are a myriad of people places in a park, many of which you will think of yourself. One area, however, that most persons do not think about checking is the sidewalk shoulders that run around a park. Or they fail to consider the grassy regions that are outside the park itself. It is not much in practice any longer, but there was a time when people used to lie on the slopes outside a park and watch the cars pass by. Take a look; they may have left something there for you.

One last suggestion regarding parks: Take a drive around and see where the grass has been freshly cut. You might just as well take advantage of the work done by the park's ground crew. Working in short grass is much easier, and every fraction of an inch that you can get your detector head closer to the ground is to your advantage.

Schools

Schools are a challenge. Coins are there in abundance, but so is metallic paper. One soon learns the difference, and once the hunter can define the difference, he does a lot less unnecessary digging. More than likely you will find nothing of real value at a school, but it is a good place to get practice, mainly because the action is fast and furious.

There is something soul-satisfying about coming up with a handful of coins the first several times out. Once a person becomes accomplished, he tends to become more selective.

Churches

Although schools yield things of little value, church grounds often have real treasure beneath the surface. It is not uncommon to find jewelry and some good coins. The dates should start at about the time the church was erected.

And related to churces are the grounds used regularly by evangelists. The area that was covered by the tent is a coin mine.

Beaches

A person does not have to live near the ocean to take advantage of beach detecting. Almost everyone has at least a sandy lakeshore to work. The yield on a beach can be the best of all with rings, jewelry, coins, and whatever else people seem determined to bury inadvertently in the sand.

For some reason lakefront beach areas are seldom worked, and the treasure is waiting for you. But even oceanfront beaches that are worked frequently provide good yields because people are just careless.

I met a young man at Fort Lauderdale, Florida, detecting on one of the public beaches there. The young man explained that Monday was his day for the beach coinshooting. The beach usually was not crowded on Monday, and after a busy weekend he figured his chances for reaping were the best.

As he and I walked along, the young man found coin after coin, all shallow and all new. I accompanied him to his car where I saw him empty his finds into a cigar box in the trunk. He must have had $25 in coins at face value in that box, as well as a gold ring.

He told me that it had been a bad morning, saying that he had found as many as six rings in a single outing. If what I saw was really just from a single outing, the anonymous young man would probably rank as one of the champion coin finders!

Stream Beds and Gold Nuggets

For persons who live in western states one of the most popular facets of metal detecting is shooting for gold nuggets. This can be a waste of time without doing your homework regarding a search area. Gold is where you find it, but if the potential does not exist, don't bother.

However, if gold has been found in the area in the past, then you have a chance. To narrow down the chance factor, look to the dry wash areas such as creeks or river beds that are occasionally the recipients of a lot of water. After a cloudburst, there is a possibility that gold has been washed down from somewhere else.

Once the search area has been selected, set your detector on its mineral sensitivity position. What you are looking for is black sand deposits.

The sand is normally highly magnetic, and the gold, if there is any, is usually found under the sand. Clear as much of the sand away as possible and reset your detector to metal. After doing that, retune it.

Work very slowly and investigate any small change in sound. Gold is heavy and will often settle in the curve of the stream. Then, too, any crevice is a natural hiding place.

Other Places to Search

Our guest experts will take you to forts, ghost towns, and battlefields, and into the old swimming holes. What we're suggesting is the more mundane places such as fair and circus grounds, the sites of annual picnics such as those given by the American Legion, the Grange, the VFW, and unions. Then, too, almost every small town has in it an abandoned railway station that offers good pickings.

And for the nickel hunters, may we suggest the grassy areas around parking meters. You may not strike gold, but there is a good chance that you will find enough for an hour's parking.

13
Flight of the Wild Goose Chase and How to Avoid It

Mention the word *research* to most persons, and it is as if you had confronted them with a snake, or a history book. But Roy and I both know that research sometimes can be as exciting as reading a mystery novel or as satisfying as fitting together a complicated picture puzzle. Nothing is quite as rewarding as finding that piece of evidence that either leads you to a cache or convinces you that the cache was never anything more than an intriguing myth.

Almost everyone interested in treasure has read about the fabulous cache that is supposed to be buried on Oak Island in Nova Scotia. Evidence of a pit was found in 1795 next to an oak tree with a lopped branch, so the story goes. As the searchers dug, they found oak planks at intervals of ten feet to a depth of about one hundred feet.

One dig after another was undertaken. Other searchers discovered that tunnels had been dug from the sea so that, if someone happened upon the pit and dug, the tide waters would fill the hole and prevent anyone from probing further.

Nothing tangible has ever been found to support the belief that treasure ever existed in the pit itself, yet treasure hunters have been so intrigued by what they think is there that they have been digging and shoveling millions of dollars into the search all these years.

It does not seem to occur to them that, if the magnificent engineer who constructed the tantalizing pit and then harnessed the tides to protect it did indeed put treasure into it, he might have returned to claim it as well. So one person after another has been scooping out holes in the island and discovering nothing.

No one seems to have bothered to do research to find out what might be or what might have been in the pit. Each, without taking into consideration the mistakes of his predecessors, just assumes that anyone who went to so much trouble to construct such a puzzle must have been hiding something very precious indeed.

What they fail to ask themselves is who did it, and why, and when, and how. All they want to know is what he put into the pit. If they did ask themselves all these things and would go to the trouble to discover the answers, they probably would not waste the time or the money to buy a shovel.

One of the things you will learn once people know you have a metal detector is that most everyone has a treasure story. At a dinner party with a half dozen guests, three will know approximately where a treasure is buried.[1] Some of the stories have validity, and common sense will tell you which ones. When you happen on one that appears worth pursuing, and it is a puzzle, that is where the fun begins.

One of the most obvious sources for information compiled in a chronological fashion is the local newspaper. However, most newspaper morgues are not open to the public for the very good reason that newspapers are in the business of putting out the news of the day and have to rely themselves on their files for research.

Yet newspapers are available in most public libraries. In these days of microfilming records, the research is made easy because an entire month or more of a newspaper may be on one small spool.

However, everything does not make the newspapers, and the thing that may interest you the most might not be a news story at all.

Perhaps what you want to know is where a town or a house once was or who lived in a particular house and when. That is when local historical societies come in handy. Often with a particularly interesting house they will have the entire chronological history. With facts, logic, and a little imagination, you can have a very rewarding solution to what began as just an intriguing puzzle. But in all stories of buried treasure, remember that the person who did the burying might have returned to recover the treasure himself. Might have!

There are books on treasure hunting, some of which are reliable guides inasmuch as they are not dramatic versions of myths. There are others that are filled with marvelous tales of things that might

1. See Chapter 13.

have happened. However, one never knows.

A German archeologist by the name of Heinrich Schliemann found the ancient city of Troy, several in fact, one on top of the other by following Homer's *Iliad*. Until that time, most scholars thought the Homeric stories were just myths.

Roy with his wonderful intuition for finding shiny things discovered one lead in tracking down a Missouri treasure in the Library of Congress in Washington, D.C. I seem to haunt historical societies and sites, museums, libraries, and more recently the offices of the Army Corps of Engineers, and the state geological surveys.[2]

A word of caution regarding the purchase of information: Maps with "X marks the spot" on them will bring treasure only to the seller.

Research often leads the seekers onto unusual paths, as it did with our next guest author, James W. Walker. Jim, an engineer with McDonnell Douglas Aircraft, measures his treasure in adventure, and he seeks it in the desert and mountain wilderness of Arizona.

What started as a hobby in metal detecting has led him to become a field expert in tracking down the sites of major and minor battles between the Indians and the United States Cavalry.

2. See Chapter 26.

14
Little Wars Found
by James W. Walker

Occasionally someone asks, "How does one get so involved in history that he is willing to spend time, money, and a great deal of energy retracing the steps of some minor event?" My answer is that it is an acquired taste. At least, it was in my case.

Seeking out sites of skirmishes between the Indians and government forces in Arizona was something in which I became interested over a period of years. There was nothing premeditated about it.

Millions of persons have been struck by the rugged beauty of Arizona and I was no exception. When passing through the state for the first time in the late 1940s, the wide open spaces were so captivating that at my first opportunity, I returned for a week to backpack through the sandy wastelands in the north. At first I would go there on vacations; then whenever I had a three-day weekend.

After a few years of walking over the northern part of Arizona, I moved south. It was then that I began finding arrowheads, old cartridge cases, military buttons, and other artifacts. These prompted curiosity about their origin, and I began acquiring a library of pamphlets and reference manuals on weapons and uniforms.

It did not take too long to realize that I was coming across scattered evidence of some kind of military engagements. Once that took hold, I was no longer visiting Arizona just for backpacking trips; I was going out to look for historical sites.

About 1955 I purchased my first metal detector. It was a cumbersome affair with a large head and weighed about fourteen pounds. If I happened to locate a place where I suspected there were a lot more artifacts beneath the surface than on top, I would take the trouble to pack it in. Subsequently, I have purchased better and lighter models, and a detector is now a constant companion on all field trips.

I began researching and, without realizing it, was becoming an authority on artifacts. Much of the reference material I was acquiring was from the Guidon Bookstore in Scottsdale, a suburb of Phoenix. The bookstore is kind of a hangout for people like myself, and it was there that I had the good fortune to hear of Dan L. Thrapp, a journalist from Los Angeles who had written several books on the conquest of the Arizona Indians.

Dan had worked from a different point of view. Whereas I was finding historical sites and then trying to learn the background of what I had found, Dan had done the research first and was trying to locate the sites at which events took place.

Our coming together was sort of a natural fusion of the researcher and the field man. In fact, it was from one of his books that I took the material for a classic discovery of a little known event that probably made absolutely no difference to history at all. But, for me, this is like a mountain to a climber. It's a challenge. It's also my way of touching the past.

The event occurred in mid-January of 1877. By this time most of the Apaches had been put on reservations. However, there were still a number of renegades roaming free who occasionally slipped onto the reservations to try to persuade their more peaceful brothers to break out and flee to the vastness of the Sierra Madres in Mexico.

In 1877, a punitive expedition was organized to round up three Tonto Apache warriors and three women who had left their reservation. The expedition was led by Major George M. Brayton in charge of ten cavalrymen, a civilian guide, and twenty-two Indian scouts. The detachment had started from old Camp Verde on the Verde River, about thirty-five miles from the site of the action.

Nine of the scouts were sent ahead of the cavalrymen to look for signs of the runaways and shortly came upon the camp of a larger number of hostiles. The scouts immediately attacked the camp, and the surprised Apaches fled to a cave nearby. Brayton brought up the remainder of his party and laid siege to the trapped Indians and for two days the fight was a stand-off.

The cave was in the side of a mesa about 1,000 feet above the floor of the canyon that ran in front of it. The top of the mesa was at about 1,800 feet. For the first 1,000 feet, the sides sloped at about a sixty-degree angle. From that point on, the face was sheer. The cave was about ten feet above the point where the sheer face joined the slope.

Seemingly a cave of this nature could be easily defended against an army by a dozen men. However, although the Apaches had food, water, and plenty of ammunition, their position was precarious. Their cave, which had two chambers separated by a small wall, had no natural fortifications such as boulders. The scouts and the cavalrymen concentrated their fire on the ceiling of the cave with telling results.

·After two days in temperatures that hovered around freezing, four of the Apaches had been killed. One of the casualties was the leader of the band, Eskeltsetle, who was infamous for luring settled Apaches away from the reservations. After he was killed, the fight went out of the rest, and they surrendered on the third day of the skirmish.

Brayton, in his detailed report, described the site of this mini-battle as being in a canyon six miles from the junction of the Verde River with the East Verde River. There were a few other details, but not enough to give a person any feeling of assurance in pinpointing the spot. The fact that the fight had occurred in a cave and not in open country justified an attempt to locate it.

Brayton did describe some of the topography, and I had learned that an aerial survey had been made of the area in the early 1950s. So, with the aid of aerial photographs and, by this time, nineteen years of experience of trekking through Arizona, I felt I had at least a chance of finding the site.

The first time I tried was in May 1966. By the time I found it, it was May 1969. But I came closer than I realized on the first trip. Unfortunately, I also came close to being permanently lost and had to be rescued by a helicopter sent from Luke Air Force Base.

When I first approached Dan Thrapp about looking for the cave, he was somewhat skeptical of ever finding it. While he passed up the initial attempt, he was along on most of the subsequent efforts. On the first trip, I was accompanied by a St. Louis acquaintance and Phil Van Strander, an architectural supply salesman from Phoenix. There would have been an invaluable fourth member with our group, Jim Blackburn, sheriff of Pine, Arizona, but official duties kept him from accompanying us. As a cowboy in the 1930s, Blackburn had become completely familiar with the country we wished to search. He was an indispensable guide on all but our first expedition.

The boulder-strewn countryside in which the Brayton-Apache fight occurred in January 1877 is enough to make a tenderfoot out of even an experienced backpacker. And the St. Louisan who was with Van Strander and me on that first trip was far from being experienced. Confronted with ninety-degree temperatures and very rugged country, it did not take him long to decide to sit and wait to be picked up on the way back.

Van Strander had years of hiking experience in Arizona, but he also had a bad knee, and after a time hiking over this never-level terrain, it began troubling him and he, too, decided to stop.

With my experience in the Arizona countryside, I should have known that this was to be a wasted trip. However, a great deal of effort and research had gone into this attempt, and I thought I would try for an hour or two longer just to see if by some stroke of good fortune I would stumble on the cave.

The topography of Arizona is dangerously deceptive. It looks very distinctive when you first see something; then when you find yourself suddenly lost, everything begins to look the same.

When I left Van Strander, I made my first big mistake. We had brought everything we could possibly need on the trip, including walkie-talkies. The first walkie-talkie we had left with the St. Louisan so we could keep in communication with him. I left not only the other walkie-talkie with Van Strander, but my entire pack as well, taking with me two cameras, a canteen, a pistol, and whatever I had in my pockets.

Trying to find the mesa that held our cave, we had followed a dry stream bed into a maze of parallel canyons. My second mistake occurred when I ignored the dry feeder streams that periodically emptied into the main channel I was following. In the direction in which I was walking, it did not appear that I would have any problem retracing my steps. If I had looked back occasionally, I would have seen the trouble into which I was falling. There would be many routes from which to choose on the way back. I never got the chance to choose, however, becoming lost long before that.

It was about five o'clock when I realized that I would be spending the night alone and without the comfort of a sleeping bag. I camped in front of the mesa that held our cave, but I wouldn't know that for another three years.

Building a fire, I prepared for what turned out to be the most miserable night I have ever spent. As the temperature dropped into the thirties, I wrapped myself around the flames, but never once stopped shivering. Without my pack I was not prepared to spend the night in the open.

The next morning I climbed to the top of an adjacent mesa, hoping that from above I would be able to orient myself so that I could make it back to our camp where I hoped my friends would be waiting.

They were waiting, but at the time they were none too friendly. They had no idea that I was in trouble and going through their minds was the thought that I had found the cave and was gathering all the artifacts for myself.

When I reached the top of the mesa, I spotted the East Verde River, but it was dry and I did not recognize it from the abundance of other dry streams in the region. Everything else looked the same. I was lost. One of the things that Blackburn had told us when it turned out that he could not come along was that if we got lost, to stay put. The local rescue team, which he headed, would come in and bail us out. I decided to stay put.

Yet I was not going to do nothing. So I built a fire, hoping that someone would see the smoke. Unfortunately, the wind dissipated the smoke quickly. Realizing that the energy I was putting into keeping the fire alive was wasted, I huddled in the shade of a juniper tree during the heat of the day, constantly harrassed by swarms of gnats.

An Air Force Rescue 43 helicopter sent to pick up James Walker from atop a mesa in Arizona.

Late in the afternoon I found out that the shaggy bark of the juniper trees would readily ignite and that the foliage burned like a flare, lasting for about five minutes. Then the smoke from the smoldering tree would pall over the mesa for hours. My friends who had waited for me all day saw the burning trees that second evening and finally realized that I was in trouble. They drove to Pine, getting Blackburn out of bed at 1:00 A.M.

The next morning, Blackburn, not knowing my condition, called out the rescue team and requested a rescue helicopter from Luke Air Force Base. Later in the afternoon, the helicopter arrived carrying a pilot, a copilot, crew chief, pararescueman, and a forest ranger, who feared that a forest fire was taking place on top of the mesa.

When the cave was ultimately found in 1969, our party was composed of Blackburn, Thrapp, Van Strander, his son, Dick, and myself. I spent considerable time searching the ground in front of the cave with my metal detector. The search yielded dozens of .50/70 cartridge cases. Inside, we found the bones of the Apaches who had been killed. We also found bits of their clothing and remnants of the bullets that had been fired into the cave.

The cave ceiling, studded with bullets, which failed to ricochet, quickly told us what Major Brayton's strategy had been.

This kind of find is not treasure, but I treasure the experience. The gold and silver for me is the days and weeks I spent in the search, the importance of which is difficult to communicate to someone who has not enjoyed one similar.

15
The Unexpected Treasure and How to Keep It

No one can take an experience like Jim Walker's away from him. However, gold and silver is another thing, as Dick and I can testify.

At one point in your treasure-hunting future, someone will ask a favor. You will be called on to find a ring or some other lost object such as a car key or something purposely buried such as a water pipe. The lost-and-found department of a treasure hunter's life just happens; he does not usually seek it out.

Some of these jobs can be rewarding in more ways than one. A person is not likely to charge a friend for help, but it is not always a friend who comes to you. If you are being hired, you should be paid. But friend or not, it should be understood beforehand that anything else found on the property should be divided on at least a fifty-fifty split.

Verbal agreements are fine, but sometimes people have short memories. A written agreement on a prepared form, signed by the landowner, eliminates squabbles if something valuable turns up. It might even save a long-standing friendship.

As an example, an acquaintance was contacted by two of his friends. The wife had lost a $1,500 ring and the treasure hunter was asked to help find it. He was successful, but in the process of the search he uncovered a second ring. It was nine inches beneath the surface.

The woman, who by this time had had her property returned to her, asked to see the second find, a man's gold ring, engraved and set with a large diamond and several smaller ones. It was obviously very old.

59

The happy treasure hunter good-naturedly handed it over to the woman to examine. That was the last he saw of the ring. She promptly put it in her pocket, declared it was hers because it had been found on her lawn, and that is where the conversation ended.

The treasure hunter lost not only his find and his time, but a friend as well. He was so angry at what had happened that he probably will never think of that couple on good terms again.

Yet he has no one to blame but himself. There was no prior agreement, and the woman was correct when she said that the ring was found on her property and therefore belonged to her.

No reward was offered for either find, and that was bad form on the part of the couple who had asked the treasure hunter for the favor. However, treasure, even small treasure, does strange things to people.

Governments, too, have acted without honor once a treasure has been uncovered. Men have spent years, not to mention a lot of money, and have undergone dangers to find a lost treasure, only to have it stolen from them by some governmental bureaucrat perfectly willing to bend the laws to suit his own greedy purpose.

But on a smaller scale, imagine what it would be like to be hired to search for a water pipe or a lost keepsake on someone's property, and as you are searching, you discover a container filled with old coins. It has happened.

An agreement ahead of time—not after—should be spelled out. Coins are easy to divide. If there are a lot of them, they can be arranged according to value by one person who then gives the other person the first choice. Once the second person chooses, the two people continue taking turns until the coins are equally divided.

However, a single item such as a ring cannot be split so easily. Yet a division can be made and very simply, too. Take two pieces of paper. On one you write your dollar bid for the item. On the other, the landowner places his bid.

Once this is done the bids are compared. The highest bidder gets the recovered item and he pays the price that the lower bidder put down on paper. It is the one way to keep everyone happy. The low bidder gets what he thought the item was worth, and the higher bidder pays less than his own estimation of the item's value.

16
The Care and Feeding of a Coin and How to Turn a Dime into a Dollar

There are coins that will bring the finders thousands of dollars as coin auctioneer Hans Schulman told you in Chapter 3. However, on the other side of the coin, there are those worth much less, though far more than their face value. This chapter is intended to help you get the most for your nickels and dimes.

Most persons, when they begin coinshooting, are satisfied just making finds. They will put them in glass jars and occasionally show them to friends as the collection begins to mount up, but the time will come when you will want to know exactly what you have. One of the best ways to find out is by using a volume such as R. S. Yeoman's *A Guidebook of United States Coins*, which can be purchased in most coin shops.

The Yeoman book is an illustrated catalogue that lists coins from 1616 to the present. It also lists prices and methods of grading.

However, a coin is worth only as much as someone is willing to pay for it, and to get the best price, one has to care for a coin and put it into its best possible condition.

Silver coins minted before the mid-1960s almost always come out of the ground in good condition. Newer coins tarnish quickly and are seldom worth more than face value.

Wash the silver off in clean water and store in folders. The folders will keep the coins from being accidentally scratched and will make it easier for you to catalogue.

Nickels are seldom found in good condition. Even if the dates and markings are plain, there are few nickels that will bring decent prices from collectors. There does not seem to be a satisfactory way of cleaning them either.

However, one-cent coins are a different story. Most old ones come out of the ground almost unidentifiable. Dealers will tell you not to clean a coin because it loses its value. Yet I've been successful in cleaning old one-cent pieces by soaking them in baking soda and water for periods of four to six days.

The warning about cleaning coins is the fear that they will be scratched. Scratches on a coin, even if the coin is very old, will reduce its book value. This is the biggest objection to using a probe such as an ice pick or a screwdriver to pry a coin out of the ground.

Coin finders often become coin collectors. However, for those more interested in dollars than in dimes, there are ways of obtaining a fair price for your merchandise. Collectors are bargain hunters, but they will pay a premium for the unusual. The idea is to let the maximum number of people know that what you have is unusual.

The best way is to advertise in a local newspaper under the "Miscellaneous for Sale" column. This should attract collectors from all parts of your area.

Another way of disposing of some of your collection is by joining a coin club. Often this will give you the opportunity to display coins on a coin shop bid board. Frequently, bid board prices will be beyond your expectations.

Coins can be entered weekly with only a small commission to the shop owner for handling the transaction. The amount of the commission, of course, is agreed upon in advance, and is standard. However, standards change from shop to shop.

If you have a significant number of real prizes, you may want to enter a coin show and set up a booth. This could put you in touch, too, with new leads on unworked locations. People have a compulsion it seems of wanting to pass on information to treasure hunters. They seem to get a vicarious pleasure in knowing that they put you onto something that might be good.

17
Yesterday's Trash Is Today's Treasure

Treasure in the most romantic sense of the word has to do with gold and precious stones. In more mundane terms, it is anything that can be turned into cash. And people collect the darndest things.

Metal detectors are being used to find old dumps, and where there are dumps, there are bottles. An old bottle in good condition often can bring more than an old coin. An illustrated bottle book will give you an idea of the worth of your finds and tell you how to dispose of them.

Years ago railroads dated their spikes to keep track of the time in which railroad ties were in service. Ties were given a lifespan and after a certain period were replaced. These dated spikes have become collectors' items.

There also is a market for political buttons, badges, tokens, lead toys, and barbed wire. The barbed wire craze has to be one of the most unusual, but it exists.

There are many types of barbed wire and almost any western-style steak house is a potential customer. It costs very little to attach foot-long lengths of different kinds of wire to a wooden plank. Attractively done, the plank and the wire become a work of art—in the eye of some beholders. The aesthetic value of this escapes us. However, we do understand the value of exchanging this."art" for cash, and that's what is important.

Remember that antique dealers are always interested in items of Americana. A trip into a ghost town or a visit to an abandoned homesite will almost always yield something of interest. Treasure doesn't always glitter.

Some of the most precious antiques are found in towns inhabited only by ghosts. It isn't always items found there that are so rare; it's the atmosphere and the history that surround them that make them worthwhile.

Ed Moody, a sales representative with one of the top metal detecting manufacturers in the world, has probably run a detector over more parts of the United States than any other man. His articles appear regularly in the leading treasure magazines.

It was through him that Dick and I became interested in ghost towns. We've been to a few, but we cannot speak with the authority of Ed Moody.

Ed Moody metal detecting in a Western ghost town.   (Photo supplied by Ed Moody)

18
No Ghosts Here—Just Their Money
by Ed Moody

Visualize a ghost town. What do you see? Are there false front buildings with most of the paint gone? Do you see broken windows and the swinging doors of the saloon hanging loosely from their hinges? Are tumbleweeds rolling through the town's only street? Is the big sign on the hotel rapping loudly in the wind against the pillars holding up the caved-in balcony where ladies of negotiable virtue once stood?

If that's what you see, then you are remembering a scene from a Western movie, because ghost towns such as that do not exist. If they ever existed, it wasn't for long. Vandals, careless visitors, and nature got to most of them.

That is not to say that there are no ghost towns with buildings still standing. There are. And not just out West. In almost every section of the United States there is a spot where a settlement once stood that is no longer occupied by human beings. Finding them is the trick. But like most treasures—and ghost towns are in themselves their own kind of treasure—they are not going to jump out at you. Yet a good part of the adventure is the looking.

Don't be too disappointed when you learn that what remains of most ghost towns are only traces, hints that people once lived there, loved there, had children there, and died there. For all the human occupation you might discover nothing more than a few rows of mortared stone—just the foundations of a town where even the buildings are ghosts.

Out West there is a certain ease in pinpointing an area where men once erected dwellings as they mined for precious metals. For instance, on the east side of the High Sierras in the Death Valley area there were a lot of silver mines. Once the mines played out, these places were abandoned. This is the kind of site the ghost towner will seek out.

If a town is marked on a map and can be easily reached by Jeep, then it probably has been stripped, at least of its obvious souvenirs. Yet if we regard each spot, even those readily accessible, as sites once occupied by man and not just as places, then there is a chance of finding something.

It is the psychology of the men that has to be assessed. Where, for instance, would a man keep his money in a town with no banks? It is not likely that he would have carried a lot of coins with him everywhere he went. So he would have to find a hiding place.

Try to analyze what you might do in a similar circumstance. Would you hide your money under a floorboard, in a wall, or out in the yard within view of the window so you could keep an eye on it?

Obviously, if you hid it, you would want to be able to find it again and be able to get to it easily. So you would probably pick out a marker such as a tree or a boulder and then bury your cache in a metal box just a few inches beneath the surface. After all one doesn't want to dig too deeply to make deposits or withdrawals.

With that in mind, the treasure hunter can stand in the doorway, or what once was a doorway of a building, and quickly plan his search. Check around the immediate outside area of the building first. Where there are or where there were windows, there is a possible find just below. Women often take their rings from their fingers to do dishes. A ring laid on a sill might easily find its way to the ground.

And if there were women in these camps, then one has to think of the possibility of where she might hide a cache, for example, in a place where she is always digging such as a flower garden around the house. A hiding place, after all, could not be obvious to passersby. And passersby in those days did not have metal detectors.

Those are the easy ones, but the rules of human psychology apply no matter where you search. Yet everyone wants to investigate a virgin area, on a site where perhaps no one has set foot for a century. To be in a place that is virtually inaccessible, enveloped in beauty shared only by the trees and the animals and wrapped in an unpolluted sky, that is what the ardent ghost towner seeks.

There are a number of good reasons for such a quest. The obvious one, of course, is that, in a place untouched, the treasure hunter has a better chance of finding a treasure. There are a number of remote ghost towns in the mountains of the northern Mother Lode area of California.

It takes some research to find and pinpoint them, and the best place to start is in the state archives or with a local historical society. Once one is located that shows some promise, prepare for the trip as you would for any remote area: food, water, compass, and all the supplies you would need for any backpacking expedition, including a pamphlet on how to survive in the outdoors. You may never need it, but it is good to have in case you do.

Looking at snow-capped peaks from the warmth and safety of a valley can mesmerize a person into believing that beauty will conquer all. But it won't.

Some years ago I heard of a ghost town called Scales in the High Sierras. There was a placer mine there from about 1850 to 1888, until a law was passed that forbade the use of hydraulic dredges in working a gold mine. Placer mining is strip mining for gold. After the law was passed, the town was abandoned.

Scales is nine miles from the nearest road, and one has to travel about forty miles on that until reaching the nearest paved highway. It is completely isolated.

It is now privately owned and is being preserved. However, at the time I went there it was not.

At its height, Scales had about 200 miners living there. They must have been a chummy bunch because in winter the town gets buried under sixteen feet of snow.

The first time I visited Scales, I was accompanied by one other man. It was spring and it seemed safe enough to travel. By the time we reached the town, which is still pretty much intact, we had walked over some fairly rough country, and admittedly we were tired.

I would like to have stayed there for a few days searching,

Volker and Paul Richmond, Dick's son, searching for coins in a ghost town in Illinois.
(Dick Richmond Photo)

but any thoughts of that were cut short when it started snowing. It took us a half day to get out of there.

Others have not been so lucky. I know of expeditions that have been trapped by sudden snows.

Later, however, I did return to Scales in summer and found, among other things, canned fruit in old fruit jars. They were in a collapsed bunkhouse.

And speaking of fruit jars, dumps in ghost towns can often provide a person with some unusual treasures in the form of bottles for the collector. It's here, too, that the detector can be a very handy tool. Certain old bottles can bring unbelievable prices, which may seem incredible to a coin man. However, beauty is in the eye of the beholder, and if an item can be turned into ready cash, that's beautiful.

In terms of beauty, I hate to mention a friend who found a number of oxshoes in a ghost town and sold them as artifacts for $1,000. I *hate* to mention it because *I* probably would have passed them up as being worthless. But one never knows.

Just as a person never knows what he will find and where. Ghost towning in California I came upon an old stagecoach road. As I followed it, it occurred to me as I came into a man-made clearing that this might have been a rest stop.

With my metal detector I found an 1880 half-dollar, a powder horn that was two feet under the surface, and five dumps. From the dumps I extracted bottles, one of which was a milk bottle on which the name of the dairy was embossed. I sold it for ten dollars. It's ridiculous when you think about it—a ten-dollar deposit for a milk bottle.

19
Inside Story
by David Hoy

Author's note: Roy and I have had the pleasure of David Hoy's friendship for a number of years and his companionship on a number of expeditions in search of sunken treasure. Dr. Hoy, an authority on extrasensory perception, is an author, lecturer, and a national personality on radio and television. His ability with ESP has been written about extensively, including the times he has discovered sunken ships using his mental capacities. He is also an adventurer. But the highest tribute Roy and I can give him is to say that he is a good shipmate. The ghosts in Ed Moody's chapter are anonymous; those in David's are of men and women who helped shape history.

• • •

Owning a metal detector would have to be a magnet for people like Roy and Dick. Their expertise has to attract people searching for things. I was no exception.

Having highly developed ESP is fine, but even at sea when I located three sunken and buried shipwrecks, it still took Roy's wizardry with the proton magnetometer to pinpoint the finds. It saved a lot of time.

I love antiques, things old and filled with dramatic history. I suppose that is part of the reason I enjoy being on expeditions with Roy and Dick. We go where few men do, and see and touch what

David Hoy searches through fireplace trash in the Gower House.   (Julius Schweich, Jr., Photo)

perhaps no one has for hundreds of years. There is a thrill in diving to the ocean floor and seeing an airlift or a prop-wash blower uncovering the remnants of a Spanish galleon. I have the feeling of grasping the past.

That's the feeling I have about an old inn I own in Smithland, Kentucky. The inn, called the Gower House, is at the confluence of the Cumberland and Ohio rivers, not too far from my home in Paducah.

Built in 1780, the fourteen-room structure gave shelter to such notables as Presidents James K. Polk and Zachary Taylor; James Audubon; Lafayette; Clara Barton, founder of the American Red Cross; Henry Clay, who held court there as a young lawyer; and Charles Dickens.

Dickens was one of several distinguished authors who stayed there. Lew Wallace, the Civil War general who was to become governor of New Mexico during Billy the Kid's time, is thought to have written part of *Ben Hur* at Gower House. And Ned Buntline, the father of the dime novel, came to Smithland to publish his works about the heroes of the West. It was Buntline who brought fame to Buffalo Bill, Wyatt Earp, and Bat Masterson.

The inn had also been in one of the opening scenes of the motion picture *How the West Was Won*.

It is now a national historic site and I am in the process of restoring it to its original condition. When I was starting, I called on Roy and Dick to help.

I pulled the floorboards out to be able to get at the foundation to strengthen it. Beneath was the dirt of almost 200 years. Brooms had swept it there in between the cracks in the floor. What else had they swept? I sensed a great deal.

Quickly my mind imagined a clutter of things. On my radio programs I'm asked hundreds of questions daily. Many of them concern lost items. I don't see things but sense where they are. I'm able to tell people with a great deal of accuracy exactly where to look. Sometimes I sense that the item is outside, which isn't much help unless they have a metal detector.

Which is exactly what I knew I needed as I scanned the earthen floors in front of me. I wasn't outside, but the principle was the same. There was a large area and everything looked similar. I was in a microcosm of ocean hunting. I needed Roy and Dick and their electronic gadgets.

They arrived with Julius S. Schweich, Jr., on a Friday night. Julius, who had been in partnership with us when we formed a motion picture company a few years back, was to photograph our finds. He did that, too, but it was his wit that made the weekend memorable. There was seldom a moment when he didn't have at least one of us laughing.

We started our search the next morning. It was rainy and cold so we spent most of Saturday working inside the inn. The outside was left until the following day.

The building was filled with little bits of metal, and at first we

David Hoy with some of the artifacts uncovered in the Gower House. (Julius Schweich, Jr., Photo)

began to think that the project would be a wasted one. I knew the three St. Louisans were interested in this site that had housed so many luminaries, but I also knew that those luminaries lose their light when a person is hunting treasure. It is only the treasure that makes them shiny again.

It seemed incredible. I thought maybe I was losing a bit of my ESP sharpness. I wondered if I had let logic get in the way of good ESP.

Then Roy found an old pair of scissors, a knife with a bone handle, and a silver thimble in the entranceway from the door facing the Ohio River. Our interest surged. Julius wanted to put down the camera and join in the hunt; he had promised his son some of the "loot" of our find. In that regard the trip was to be a frustrating one for him.

We bought a rake and a shovel and started smoothing the rough dirt surface in some of the rooms. Then Roy found an 1867 nickel in excellent condition.

Shovel and rake began to work furiously. Dick, by the way, looks natural with a shovel in his hands. I think his fingers are really too stubby for the typewriter.

By the end of the day Roy had found several other items, Dick had blisters (soft hands), Julius had some good pictures (but no coins), and I uncovered three barber quarters. I was so proud you would have thought I had found a treasure galleon.

The one room in which the floors had not been removed had been the tavern in the old inn. So the next day we ripped up the boards. Within the first thirty minutes Roy found a 1772 Spanish two real. That was a thrill because we knew that it had probably been there for almost the entire 200 years that the building had been standing.

We kept finding things one after the other: buttons and coins and small utensils. I now have them in a case at home. When the inn is restored, I'll put them on display there.

Outside was another story. We received one reading after another. Most of what we found was modern and we quickly gave up. But I own a metal detector now and I'm methodically searching the grounds. My ESP tells me that the others gave up too soon.

20
Unsolved Mystery

David would have never made that crack about my soft hands if he had seen the way Roy had me digging when we went in search of the mystery galleon.

On a stretch of Florida coastline north of Vero Beach, there is a piece of property owned by Hugh Corrigan, Jr., and his brother Pat. It is just like a lot of the snake-infested, jungle-lined beaches that separate the tourist towns on the Atlantic coast except for one thing. For years, after storms, people have been finding Spanish gold and silver on the sand.

What made this money beach particularly intriguing was that Corrigan's Beach, as it is known locally, is almost in the center of the area where the 1715 Spanish plate fleet went down.[1]

Millions of dollars have been picked from the bones of wrecks that have been found. The coins discovered on Corrigan's Beach were of the right period, and the shoreline was being seeded from somewhere.

At first it was assumed that buried in the sand somewhere offshore was one of the missing wrecks. Then about a thousand feet from the beach in eighteen feet of water, fourteen cannons were discovered. They lay in a pattern indicating that they had been tossed from a rocking ship as it was driven toward shore in a hurricane. South of Corrigan's Beach, much closer to shore, is a "hot spot" that proved to be nothing. It seemed logical that there had to be a wreck, and the water was searched electronically time and again. Except for the cannons, there seemed to be nothing else tangible.

1. See Chapters 1, 3, and 21.

Yet, storm after storm, coins were being picked up, and the blows were not always big ones. A treasure hunter flew over the beach in a helicopter. From the air, he electronically searched the area and finally got a reading, but not over the water. The electronic device he was using indicated that the ship was buried on the beach.

The company for which the treasure hunter was employed approached the Corrigans. They were not interested in the offer made. Besides that, the only treasure hunter with whom they were on friendly terms was Roy.

• • •

Dick's right, they were friendly. Over a period of years, I had discussed the possibility with them of working the wreck. However, they were not interested in having anyone dig up their beach, not even me.

Then, five years after the idea was first proposed, the Corrigans and I reached an agreement. A contract was drawn and signed.

In the winter of 1972-73, Dick and I and two of our companions on a number of underwater hunts, Don Paule and Ed Kastner, drove from St. Louis to Vero. We carried with us a proton magnetometer and all the equipment needed for a land search, including shovels. Dick was pretty unhappy about that because David's right; a shovel does look natural in his hands.

I had seen the cannons and had found the "hot spot" in the water to the south, and also had been with an outfit that had electronically searched the offshore waters. I was a friend of the man who claimed he had electronically spotted the wreck on the beach. Dick and I had seen boxes of the coins found on the beach. Before the trip was over, the others would see the coins as well.

It was the end of December when we arrived, and the first day on the beach was miserably cold. A wind was whipping up the surf, and the damp air penetrated the clothing we had brought with us.

An access road had been cut through the palmetto jungle about in the center of the Corrigan property. From the road we worked south first. Ed carried the magnetometer head, Dick and Don the batteries, me the magnetometer, reading it as we moved along.

The beach was to be searched electronically as no beach had ever

Volker reads the meters of the proton magnetometer as Ed Kastner (left) and Don Paule move the sensing head around to outline the direction that the ship took when it foundered on Corrigan's Beach.

been searched before. We moved slowly, ten feet at a time. There was a reading taken at the water's edge, at the high-water mark, at the edge of the bluff, and then into the palmetto itself.

In the more than 250 years since the ship went down, the coastline could have changed considerably. It did not seem likely that a ship would have been driven so far inshore, but in a hurricane, stranger things have happened. We were taking no chances.

For two days we searched south and in that time got just one reading. It was assumed that it was a cannon buried deep in the sand. But even if it was, one cannon does not make a shipwreck.

On the third day Dick had to drive to Orlando to meet with a motion picture producer. It was a new company intent on making G-rated movies. It had all the elements for a full-scale production company, and Dick was being considered to head the true-life adventure division of the firm, which is not bad for a guy with stubby fingers. He got the job, but as it turned out the company never quite blossomed. The millions of dollars that were coming from Europe to underwrite the firm got into some fuzzy legal entanglements.

But that is another story. The only point to it at all was that it was while Dick was gone that we found the ship.

• • •

I had driven in from Orlando early in the morning and had no idea about the apparent success of the venture. I learned at dawn when Roy, singing his rotten little good morning song, pulled me out of bed, then stood there grinning at me.

"We found it," Roy announced, in a manner of a man who had just come into an inheritance.

"Found what?" I asked sleepily.

"The ship," Don grinned.

"You're kidding!"

"That's right, Partner," Ed put in. It was not until I opened my eyes enough to see Ed fully dressed and ready to go that I realized that they were not putting me on. Ed is a man who loves sleep, and the possibility of this kind of action would be the only thing that would get him out of bed so early.

Ten minutes later we were in a nearby grocery buying supplies for the day. There would be no lunch breaks the rest of the time in Florida. From dawn to dusk we would be checking and rechecking the find, charting it, checking the surf, then moving on to search the rest of the beach.

By the fourth day the weather had warmed up considerably, and for the four of us who had just moved down from the bitter cold of a St. Louis winter, it seemed like summer. Work was done in jeans or just swimming trunks.

The wreckage was north of the road. Roy first picked up indications of it at the water's edge one hundred feet north. The readings got hotter and hotter before trailing off and returning to normal in the next one hundred feet. In the same area at the high-water mark it was hotter still. At the edge of the jungle the reading of the magnetometer went absolutely insane.

We went over it again and again, marking readings on a grid. To complete the pattern, which, by the time the job was over, would show the classic route of a ship to its final resting place, Don and Ed donned wet suits and carried the magnetometer head into the water. This was no mean task since the water was murky, choppy, and filled with sharks. More often than not, the men would lose their footing, get dunked, and have to renew their efforts.

The pattern was perfect. At sea we had seen this type of thing time and again when we found wrecks. The trailings came right out of the water, stopping at the bank that marked the edge of the jungle. The wreckage of a ship was there; there was no doubt about it.

But how deep?

In spite of those crude remarks made by my two "friends" about my hands fitting a shovel, I want to state flatly that I was against digging. Nevertheless, I dug.

Don and Roy were intent on finding out how deep. Ed had brought along a bore to test the depth of the bedrock beneath the sand. We knew at a thousand feet offshore, where the cannons were in eighteen feet of water, bedrock was three feet beneath the sand.

As I mentioned earlier, before traveling to Florida the project had been discussed with a civil engineer who had consulted a geodetic survey of the area. If the pattern of the bedrock ran true to form, high on the beach we figured we could reach it at twenty-five feet. Was it possible to dig down twenty-five feet by hand?

"No!" I insisted, and was handed a shovel.

The bore was pounded into the sand. At a depth of fifteen feet, at the hottest spot in the search area, it could not be driven an inch further. We had hit something. We were sure of it.

For an entire day we dug. At twelve feet the sand got wet. The bore was tried again, but this time we were stopped after a few feet. The wet sand, we discovered, packed around the bore, preventing us from pounding it deeper. It had not been bedrock that had stopped us after all.

The digging had been a waste of time. At least that is what we thought. If we had dug at a spot ten feet closer to the water, we would have saved ourselves another trip to Florida and a considerable amount of money.

Frustrated, we returned to St. Louis. We knew for sure what we had taken for granted all along; if the wreck was to be uncovered, it would take a dragline to do it. Roy had a problem.

Everything indicated that a ship had been wrecked on Corrigan's Beach and the trick was to see just how far down it was. In an unsuccessful effort to dig their way to it, Richmond (glasses) and Ed Kastner put the shovels to work. (Roy Volker Photo)

• • •

Dick and I knew before we left Florida that there would be no dragline available to us in Vero that could be used without arousing gossip of a treasure hunt. So I contacted Tory Dowsett, a friend in Miami. Tory found a man willing to haul a dragline to Vero from Miami, and the dragline operator and I struck a bargain.

Everything sounds simple except when you are in the process of doing it. Don and two of his associates drove down from St. Louis to set up camp on the beach and to block off the access area to trespassers. Also they were to meet the dragline operator and direct him to the site.

Ken White, Jr., of White Electronics, and his wife Myrna had driven in from Tampa, where they were having a diving boat built.

Ken's firm had developed a new low-frequency metal detector, and this was to be his opportunity to test it. The Corrigans had rearranged their business plans to be on hand. Dick, Ed, and I flew in with Julius Schweich, who was to photograph the operation.

The flight south should have been an indicator of what we could expect from the entire operation. The plane was caught in a storm and it bumped around in the sky over Atlanta for more than an hour. We changed planes in Atlanta for a flight to Melbourne, Florida.

We were late in landing and even later catching the next available flight out. So when we finally did arrive in Melbourne, the airport terminal was about to close.

Don and his associates were there waiting with the news that the dragline operator had not arrived. The project was to be a weekend operation unless we hit it big, and we didn't have that much time. So the next two hours were spent on the telephone trying to locate our dragline operator.

Dick's years as a newspaperman really came in handy. He called the city desk of the *Miami Herald*, the Florida telephone company, and the police department of a small town, and finally ran down the dragline operator's telephone number at home. This problem would have been avoided had Tory still been in Miami. He had, however, been called out the day before on an underwater demolition job.

At 4:00 A.M. we finally reached the dragline operator, who told us simply that he had not yet received my check. The certified check had been sent three days earlier airmail special delivery. Yet the man was not convinced. No check, no dragline.

Dick and I checked our wallets and saw we had enough to pay the man in cash if he would just drive to Vero with his equipment.

● ● ●

I could tell as I stood listening to the one-sided phone conversation that Roy was having trouble convincing the man of his sincerity. But Roy can be very persuasive. When the dragline operator finally agreed on a cash-on-delivery proposition, Roy let him go back to sleep. Too much was riding on the unhappy fact that the man's mail was late in arriving.

Early the next morning Roy was again on the phone to Miami. The man had finally received the check, but now he was having other problems; the flatbed truck that he used to haul the dragline had broken down and he was going to have to find a replacement.

It was Saturday and morning became afternoon and afternoon approached evening. Still there was no sign of the missing dragline man. It was going to be too late. Hundreds of dollars would be blown on a wasted trip and still no one would know what had been found.

Then a dragline arrived. We thought it was ours and almost had it off the truck before the driver discovered his mistake. With that, the waiting suddenly became unbearable. Roy had spotted a dragline nearby and went to negotiate another deal. To hell with secrecy.

I took off in a car, heading for Miami to see if I could locate the missing man. Just as I reached one of the main intersections in Vero, I found the dragline operator from Miami parked alongside the road. He was lost.

I quickly gave him directions, then wheeled the car around to rush back and try to intercept Roy before he was forced to spill the beans to the new dragline man about what we were up to on Corrigan's Beach. It was too late. But Roy in his marvelous imagination told the new man that we were part of a scientific expedition trying to uncover a meteorite. The man probably did not believe him, but at that point everyone was so happy to get the project underway we didn't care what he thought.

By the time the dragline was unloaded and had been driven up to the spot where the buried ship had been discovered on the previous trip south, the sun was low in the sky. But the huge shovel began to gobble up the beach quickly and I was sure we would know what was there before dark.

• • •

But Dick was wrong. It was well past sunset when the dragline operator, working by a single oil lamp, lifted the timbers out of the ground. The excitement was incredible but brief. I knew immediately what had been found was not the remains of a Spanish galleon

A dragline fills in the hole that it dug at Corrigan's Beach after it was discovered that the wreck found was less than 100 years old.   (Julius Schweich, Jr., Photo)

but that of a ship of a much later date. If disappointment could be measured like a blow to the stomach, that sight almost put me down for a nine count. The treasure wreck on the beach was a myth. To learn the truth had cost me and my associates a considerable amount of time, effort, and money.

But that is not the end of the story. As a matter of fact, it could just be the beginning. The next day Myrna White, using a small metal detector, found a four-real Spanish piece-of-eight near the area where the dig took place.

The treasure is not on the beach, but is washing up from

(Julius Schweich, Jr., Photo)

Myrna White holds a two-real Spanish coin that she found on Corrigan's Beach in the area where Volker, Richmond, and company dug for a galleon.

someplace in the surf between the cannons and the shoreline. But the wreck, if there is a wreck, cannot be detected in the ordinary way. It still intrigues me.

Our next guest writer, Sam A. Staples, started out on the beach like we did, and resolved his problem. He is now part of the best-equipped treasure-hunting outfit in the United States.

21
Gold and Silver Fruit
by Sam A. Staples

Single-minded? Probably. But I've been accused of worse. Besides I don't think that dedication to an idea is a fault, especially now that I'm beginning to see years of labor starting to bear gold and silver fruit.

Becoming part of the best-equipped treasure-hunting outfit in the United States would have seemed incredible to me in 1965 when all I had was an idea and a couple of cigar boxes filled with old Spanish silver coins. And the coins were not even mine.

But it was that silver that got me interested in treasure hunting. It has consumed my life ever since. Thinking back on those first years of struggle, of working nights at Cape Canaveral and days on the beach scrounging for coins with a metal detector after storms, I have wondered if I would put myself through it again if I had the chance. There was darn little to keep my dream alive then. I never answer, but in my heart I'm aware that the answer is never no.

It was an old man by the name of George Billie who found the coins. The dates were all 1715 or earlier. By the time I met Billie, Kip Wagner and his company, Real Eight, had already made their spectacular finds at Cabin Beach, just south of Sebastian Inlet, and at Fort Pierce. Everyone was talking treasure and I was no exception.

My job as an aircraft missile mechanical technician at the Cape seemed pretty tame compared to the possibility of finding treasure. When I met Billie, he was working with an outfit involved in strip mining on a beach.

The mining outfit was scooping sand onto a shaker table. The table would shake the sand, keeping the high-grade material and dumping the overburden. While the overburden was being shoveled off, Billie would pick up these coins.

The beach is nine miles north of Sebastian Inlet and from this small evidence I thought that one of the ten treasure ships that sank in a hurricane on July 31, 1715, had gone down there.

So Billie and I and another man by the name of Hal Robinson joined forces. We weren't sure what we wanted to do because we had no capital. We worked the beach a couple of times after storms and found nothing. So without ever finding a single coin myself, I went looking for a backer to help support a project that must have sounded like a fantasy when I approached Jim Rathmann with it.

However, Rathmann is a man familiar with dreams and making them come true. He was a racing car driver who captured the biggest prize of all when he won the Indianapolis 500 in 1960. He had all the qualifications needed. He was a daredevil, an adventurer, a visionary, and by then a man of means. He wasn't interested.

By 1965 Rathmann was president of Jim Rathmann Chevrolet-Cadillac, Inc., an automobile dealership in Melbourne, Florida. When we approached him, he didn't seem too impressed with the project. But he is a kind man and he invited us to his home. When we arrived, Billie came bearing the two cigar boxes of silver coins and dumped the contents onto the Rathmann kitchen table. That impressed him. But it did not win him over.

However, we did come together several more times with him trying to feel us out as to what we wanted and us trying to tell him without fouling up the possibility of his joining our little group. Finally, he did join, and we decided to form a corporation called Doubloon Salvage and filed for a lease. Rathmann is the president of the corporation, which now includes nine others besides myself.

Once convinced, he has been a substantial part of the spirit that has sustained us. It has been that spirit that has induced others to join the corporation. It was Rathmann who brought in Anton Hulman, Jr., president of Indianapolis Motor Speedway: Edward N. Cole, president of General Motors; Miami attorney Richard R.

Paige; astronaut Charles Conrad; Adrian S. Hopper, president of Interstate Oil Transport Co.; Thomas R. Green, president of Dispatch Services, Inc.; Foy D. Jordan, vice president of Dispatch Services; Wilburn L. Johnson, president of Jim Robbins Co.; and Arthur W. Hartman, a diving boat captain and the operator of a marine establishment.

But those people joined us years later in the spring of 1971. We still had a lot of learning to do, and a lot of hard times. In fact, it was two years later that we were finally granted a lease. The state of Florida, in an effort to prevent wholesale lawlessness regarding treasure salvaging, is very careful to whom it grants leases.

In the meanwhile we would go storm chasing, picking up hundreds of coins from the beach. One evening after a storm, using a metal detector, I found ninety coins in forty-five minutes. At the same time, Rathmann's wife Kay found about sixty. All were the irregularly shaped cob coins, some from the late 1600s. None later than 1715.

Also we purchased a boat, the 39-foot *Hal-Mar*, and outfitted it.

Sam Staples (left) and Art Hartman aboard the diving boat *Arto*.

(Dick Richmond Photo)

A prop-wash blower was designed to blow the sand off the wreck when we found it.

What we didn't know then was that we would never find a wreck, at least not a 1715 wreck, and that most of our activity for the next five years would be on the beach and in the surf just offshore.

When the lease came through in 1967, we did not own a magnetometer. Without one, we would never find anything. So we worked deals with Real Eight, Mel Fisher of Treasure Salvors, and at one time with Art Hartman, who was later to join the corporation and for a time to direct its search operations.

In all those searches with the magnetometer we found nothing. Yet the coins kept coming up out of the surf. Finally we discovered close to shore what appeared to be a small wreck. We have since surmised that it was a mail boat that sank during a layover for provisions at a hotel that once stood at Rum Cove.

At the time, however, we thought we had found the ship we had been looking for all those months. We realized that the *Hal-Mar* would not do us much good. First, the wreck was too close to shore; more important, however, was the time-consuming labor I had of sailing a boat from a safe harbor on the Indian River through Sebastian Inlet and up the coast for miles twice daily.

So we built a barge on wheels. We would launch it off the beach and run it down about 100 yards to the spot where we thought the wreck site was and go to work. It would take us about fifteen minutes to get on the beach and then to be actually on the site and digging.

The propulsion unit was a Daytona 427 engine set through a hole in the center of the barge. Over it we set a device called a mailbox, which, when it covers the propulsion unit, becomes a blower. With that we could blow the sand away down to bedrock.

We anchored the barge with permanent settings, using concrete-filled fifty-five-gallon drums set in holes. The anchor lines were tied together, and the drums were marked with buoys.

Getting on the site was easy. Getting off was no problem either. We had a winch truck onshore. When we came ashore, we would hook up the barge and winch it back onto the beach.

It did not take us long to realize that the wreck we found was neither a galleon nor Spanish, but we were certain that the wreck, our wreck, had to be somewhere in the surf. We continued to blow holes in the sand.

We found a couple of beach buggies, barrels, cans, and drums. It was very disheartening because we still were finding coins on the beach. Never once, however, did we find one in the water.

So my schedule every day for five years was to be at the Cape at 4:45 P.M. I'd get off at 1:30 A.M., and by 7 A.M. I would meet the others on the beach. I'd work until about 2:30 P.M., then I would take off for home, shave, shower and grab a sandwich to eat on the drive to my money-paying job. The beach job was costing me and the others about $5,000 apiece every year.

Although we never found anything with it, the barge provided us with our first working contact with Real Eight; by the time we were fully operational, that company had pulled millions of dollars in treasure out of the ocean. Kip Wagner wanted to work closer to the beach on his Cabin Wreck, and we thought we had a wreck in deeper water.

So, he provided us with Real Eight's magnetometer and a man to operate it, and I provided him with our barge and a man. It was a verbal agreement. Later when Doubloon Salvage expanded into a fully-equipped ocean-going outfit, we entered into written agreements with Real Eight to work its leases that stretch for miles from Sebastian Inlet south to Jupiter Inlet. It is here that the treasure fleet lies and every year we pick up more from it. Big finds have been made here, but there is more. Much more!

It all started for Doubloon when we began using metal detectors to find coins on the beach. The question: Is there a wreck undetected there somewhere? No. Even though coins are still coming out of the water to this day, we feel we can now offer several possible explanations, even though there is no wreck.

The first and perhaps the most reasonable one is that the currents carried part of a galleon and with it a few chests of silver north nine miles. Another is that what we found is from a load made by a group of original salvors. Men in small boats using grappling hooks are known to have salvaged some of the treasure in the years immediately after the fleet sank. Our silver may have come from an early salvage boat that found itself a victim of another storm,

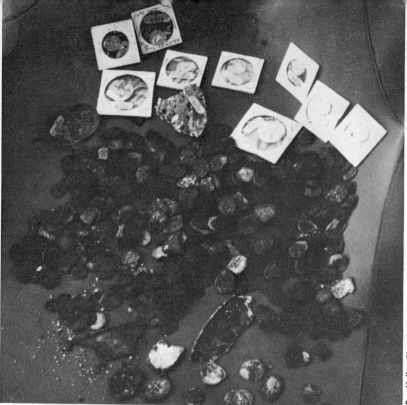

Some of the treasure found by Doubloon Salvage in Florida waters.

sinking where we were to pick up coins 250 years later.

The third explanation is less acceptable to me because of a number of reasons. This is a theory that our finds were part of a land cache. It is known that there was much looting among the survivors of the fleet. However, the suggestion that our finds might be part of that loot I find unpalatable.

First of all, our coins indicate water wear. Second, we found the coins scattered over a distance, not in a pile like in a cache.

But the more obvious reasons why I cannot digest the land theory are answered in two questions I've asked myself: Why would anyone lug heavy chests nine miles or even a half-mile when there are plenty of hiding places near the site of the wreck? How could a looter drag heavy chests across the treacherous waters of Sebastian Inlet?

The real answer as to how the silver reached our beach, we will probably never know. But I do know there is no wreck there, only the coins after a storm.

22
Treasure Fishing
by Ray Williams

Author's note: The galleons have the big treasure, but as you have read from Dick's and my experience and from that of Sam Staples, they also have the big frustrations and expenses. Ray Williams, an employee of a metal detecting manufacturer, has developed a way to pluck treasure out of the water on a low-risk basis.

• • •

A lot of people can be hot on the heels of the same treasure, and once it is found, that's it. No more treasure. In my way of looking at things, it doesn't have to be that way. There are places all over the world where, once coins and jewelry are removed by the metal detecting enthusiast, there are people who are ready to rush right in and replenish the stock.

What I'm talking about is the old swimming hole where every summer people gather to lose their valuables. They don't do it on purpose, of course, but swimmers wearing rings forget that their fingers shrink while in water and, oops!, there goes another family heirloom.

And for reasons best known to swimmers of the world, they feel obligated to carry coins with them in their swimming suits or cut-off jeans. At least, it seems that way from the number I've found.

Now that you know where, let me try to explain how, and with what.

We'll take the "with what" first. The list may seem long initially, but let me assure you that it takes longer to tell about it than it does to assemble everything after the first time.

1. Metal detector with interchangeable waterproofed loops. The loops are buoyant and a nonmetallic weight will be needed to hold them down. So nonmetallic D-rings and straps should be installed in loops to hold weights.

2. Loops come in a number of diameters. I prefer the six-inch diameter because it has better depth penetration say than a four-inch model and less buoyancy than a seven-and-a-half-inch model.

3. A float large enough to hold your detector, yet small enough so it won't be bothersome. I constructed mine of styrofoam, although a person could use an inner tube or any other floatable object.

4. A grain scoop. This can be purchased at a hardware or grain store. From the center, cut out a piece six inches square and replace it with a half-inch mesh screen. Instead of the screen, holes can be drilled in the scoop, but the screen seems to work best. It allows mud and sand to sift through, but will catch any coin, ring, or other items that might be worth keeping. Attach a five-foot wooden handle to the scoop and fasten securely with braces.

5. Waders, bathing suit, tennis shoes, flashlight with a strap attached, or a miner's head lamp conclude the gear needed.

The reason for the waders is that I usually start my water searching as soon as the ice of winter melts. The flashlight is necessary only if you happen to be as insane as I am and keep searching after dark.

Which brings up words of caution: Wearing waders at night and finding a hole or a drop-off can end one's career as a treasure fisherman. If you insist on following my example, know your swimming hole. Otherwise you might find these words engraved on your headstone: "He could not wade until morning."

In warmer weather, the waders are abandoned for tennis shoes. The shoes are worn to protect the feet from gravelly bottoms and to aid in kicking the back of the scoop to get penetration for deeper targets.

All swimming areas can be considered hot spots. Of course, the older ones will be the best. There is nothing like a chat with one of your town's senior citizens to discover where he went swimming as a boy.

Most states consider all water as public domain; if you have public access to the lake, even when the beach is on private property, it is lawful to treasure hunt in the water as long as you do not step up on the land. However, these places are best left alone unless you can get permission from the owner. There is no sense in being a pain in the lake if you have other happy hunting grounds.

One way to woo a reluctant lake owner over is to tell him you will remove the trash that you find.

When wading, tune your machine the same as you would on land. Then work the probe in the same arc pattern as you would on land.

I have found diamond rings at the water's edge and neck deep.

Ray Williams, the treasure fisherman, working a lake near his home in Indiana.
(Photo supplied by Ray Williams)

When you get a reading, keep your loop over the target until the scoop is directly in front of it. Once that is done, move the probe to one side and let go. Then with both hands pull the scoop toward your body. In areas where the bottom is hard push the scoop with your shoe.

With practice you should be able to hit the target in one or two tries. And one of the great things is that the target is not likely to be a bottle cap or a pull tab. There is much less trash in water where people swim.

Seldom have I been on a wading outing without finding at least one ring or a handful of coins. In one three-hour hunt I discovered forty dollars in coins at face value and more than thirty rings.

Most coins taken from fresh water are in good condition, although often they are dark blue in color. Some of the older silver coins will have a dark crust on them. Often if these encrusted coins are rubbed with the fingers as soon as they are taken out of the water, the covering will come off. If left to harden, the crust is almost impossible to remove without damaging the coin.

There is plenty of adventure in finding coins and rings, especially when they come in large quantities. The largest single find I've made thus far was on **February** 16, 1974. However, finding seventy-nine half-dollars at one time was not as thrilling as knowing from where they came.

I was hunting coins beneath a bridge in Christiana Creek near Elkhart, Indiana, when I got a loud signal. I had the shaft of my probe extended and the area from which I was getting the signal was in a spot that was too deep for my waders.

I tested the water with my hand. It was icy. But that signal kept calling me like a siren. I knew that to go in and get wet in those temperatures, I had to be a little crazy. Common sense told me not to, but I went regardless.

What I found was loot from a robbery at a nearby lounge. It was in a bank deposit bag, and I was shaking so bad from the cold and the excitement that I had trouble opening it. Inside were eleven checks worth about $250 and the seventy-nine half-dollars. Apparently, the coins were used to weight the bag.

I telephoned the owner of the lounge and then the police. We met and the lounge owner allowed me to keep the bank bag and the half-dollars.

A bank bag and $39.50 is not a lot of treasure, but to me it was worth the icy dip. If someone offered me $39.50 to jump in that water in February, I know I wouldn't do it. But if I thought there might be another bag in there, I'd go in waders and all.

Splash!

23
A Line Named Siegfried
by Major James C. Byrk

Author's note: A few years before Roy and I joined forces, I spent several weeks at Elgin Air Force Base, Florida, doing research for a book on the Air Force pararescuemen. One of the scores of men I interviewed was Jim Byrk, the first Air Force nurse to become qualified as a pararescueman. During my stay there we became friends and I got to know a great deal about him. He set up and taught an emergency field medicine course at the Pararescue School for three and a half years, earned his master parachutist's wings, went through the Navy scuba course, and flew on air evacuation aircraft as a flight nurse. He is also a private pilot. I also learned that a childhood interest in homemade cannons and explosives earned him a stomach wound, a burned hand, and a healthy respect for things that go "bang." Perhaps that's what led him to become a nurse anesthetist. Whatever, his interest in things historical have drawn him to dig in old ruins in New Mexico, to search the caves occupied by the retreating Japanese in the hills near Clark Air Base in the Philippines, and to use a metal detector in search of artifacts on the Siegfried Line in Germany. In researching the history of the Line, he made another discovery: the Romans dropped a lot of coins in the area.

• • •

The Siegfried Line has earned a firm place in the history of war. Stretching from Kleve in the Netherlands to Lorrach in Switzerland, this fortification of over 3,000 bunkers, pillboxes, and observation

The dragon teeth of the Siegfried Line.   (James C. Byrk Photo)

posts has seen much bloody fighting. Many middle-aged men today carry scars and memories of the Battle of the Bulge and Huertgen Forest. The Siegfried Line figured prominently in both these battles, which took place between September 1944 and January 1945.

I had just become the owner of a new metal detector when I was transferred to Bitburg Air Base in the Eifel Mountains. Bitburg is right in the middle of the Line.

Since boyhood, I've been fascinated by things military, and while attending the Air Force jungle survival school at the top of a mountain near Clark Air Base in the Philippines, I explored nearby caves. The caves in the rugged Zambales Mountains figured prominently in the last-ditch effort by the Japanese to hold out in World

War II. Much debris was left in this still-wild area, and it was not uncommon to find artifacts of the war years.

However, in Germany, which is covered with farms, most of the surface debris has been removed. A metal detector is a must.

The house in which I live with my wife and four children overlooks the Pruem River. It's about five miles from Echternach, Luxembourg, in the area that was the southern flank of the Battle of the Bulge. From the bottom of the hill where our house sits, the 212th Volksgrenadier Division pushed off in rubber rafts across the Sauer to secure that flank. Within a five-mile radius of our house, too, are over 106 bunkers of the Siegfried Line.

The United States military, as well as the German government, are understandably concerned about people becoming injured and try to discourage bunker hunting.

As a preventive measure, the bunkers have been dynamited, flooded, sealed, and buried. In spite of this, many are more or less intact. My two sons and I have explored a few out of curiosity, but the ferro-concrete construction drives a metal detector bananas. So serious searching nearby is out of the question.

An experience in my childhood has made me extremely cautious about explosives. Based on that I spent some time laying ground rules for the boys. They don't pick up anything until after I see it, and if it's loaded, or I don't know what it is, it stays untouched.

We may pass up some good souvenirs, but I want us to keep our fingers and eyes where nature meant them to be. In addition, I like to take along another adult — for insurance. So far there's been no shortage of eager volunteers.

One of our first finds, on a hill near our house, brought home my point about danger. Behind a small bunker we discovered an unexploded 105 mm Howitzer shell. It was a foot deep at the tip and angled deeper at the rear. I didn't bother to find out how much deeper, but covered it up. It's in an extremely rough overgrown area and unlikely to be disturbed again — especially by me.

We started our search in autumn and really didn't have too many good days for souvenir hunting before winter set in. But we did locate two German canteen cups, two empty concussion grenades, a number of 8 mm cartridges, and about 200 pounds of shrapnel.

During our digging, we discovered an interesting property of the German soil near here: It has more stone than dirt, and in winter becomes harder than the bunkers themselves.

During the following winter, we spent most of our free time studying the history of the Line and listening to stories of the finds of other bunker hunters. *The Official History of the Siegfried Line Campaign* by Charles B. MacDonald is an excellent source. It contains descriptions of the action sites and a number of maps, which I traced. It was after that that I discovered 1:25,000 scale topographical maps, which are sold in German bookstores. These maps have every little footpath and building marked on them, including the bunkers.

In my reading I noted that a month prior to the Bulge that a bridgehead had been established near here. In September, 1944, units of the Fifth United States Army crossed the Sauer and started toward Bitburg. Near Mettendorf, the force was slowed and it established a defensive position on Hill 407. Since I knew that the Army names the hills according to height in meters, one look at the map showed a hill 407 meters high named Auf Hasslich.

As soon as spring arrived, my boys, Mike and Doug, and I headed for Auf Hasslich. We walked up through the weeds finding a number of foxholes but nothing else. We were following what we calculated to be the path of the 108th Panzer Brigade's foot soldiers.

I kept swinging the head of the metal detector slowly as we moved. Finally, after crossing a half-mile of open fields, we got a buzz. Probing around, the needle on the meter and the buzzer went wild. We found a large number of bullets, most of which were ruptured from heat, and parts of what may have been a tank. It was all within a circle twenty feet in diameter.

We moved another hundred yards up the north slope to the ridge of trees and thornbushes that ran along the military crest of the hill. Not eager to have the thorns tear the clothes from our backs, we walked along the edge searching. Then I spotted a German 88 mm shell with the remains of resistors and wiring hanging from its broken fuse.

Bypassing it, we crawled on our hands and knees into a less dense part of the thicket. Mike, the eldest, had the detector and said he had found a pipe. I looked over to where he was and saw a brass shell casing that turned out to be a 37 mm United States shell made in 1943.

Moving on with Doug, who was complaining because we'd found only one shell, we came across three badly rusted steel Howitzer shells. The complaints stopped. At last we were finding something besides shrapnel and old oxen shoes.

While the boys carried our treasure to the edge of the weeds, I kept detecting. Suddenly the needle shot to the high end of the scale. Moving the loop around, I determined the buried object to be about three feet by six inches, give or take a foot or two.

We have no way of judging depth so I started carefully brushing back leaves before attacking the rocks with our foxhole shovel. With the leaves removed, as well as a small amount of surface soil, I saw the familiar shape of a trigger guard.

Excitedly, I called the boys, then began quickly, but carefully, brushing away the rest of the soil. Every bunker hunter I had talked to had wistfully ended his story with the hope of finding a German weapon. I couldn't believe that maybe I had. But there it was—a German machine pistol—and I had discovered it in the spot where it had lain for thirty years.

I didn't care that it was a mass of fragile rust. Had it been brand new and packed in cosmoline, I wouldn't have been happier. My boys were proud of me. After all, this had been our first outing away from the hills near our house.

We started for home, picking up a flattened German ammunition box on the way. It was getting late and we could come back and finish sweeping the ridge another time.

My long-suffering wife was as happy as we were once the trail of rust, leaves, and dirt were removed from the stairway.

Most of the things we found were discarded since they were pretty well deteriorated, but I'm trying to preserve the machine pistol by dipping it in hot paraffin. If I succeed, the gun will be mounted on a plaque with vital statistics on a brass plate below.

Heady with success, the boys and I were joined the following day by Trent Riley for a trip to Huertgen Forest. From mid-September to mid-December 1944, this huge forest was trampled by American and German troops, the seventy-foot pines shattered by tree bursts and the forest floor pitted with log-roofed bunkers.

In October 1944, the German 275th Fusilier Battalion dug in along two streams bisecting the forest. We decided to head for the valley worn by the stream, Weisser Weh.

Driving past miles of dragon's teeth and bunkers, we stopped once to buy a topographic map of the Huertgen Wald. We could only find a 1:50,000 scale, which didn't show bunkers, but we were more interested in finding the creeks and roads, which it did show.

We parked by a gate, ate lunch, and headed up a forest road paralleling the Weisser Weh. After a quarter-mile, the six-foot fence ended and we started searching a fifty-foot-wide strip between the pines and the road. We found a dozen small ammunition cartridges and a few feet further along, the foxholes began.

In the bottom of the first one, which was about six inches deep, we found several 30 caliber United States cartridges. While digging these out, we came across a snap-on goggle lens and a pocket comb. Stamped into the plastic of the comb were the words, "Made in USA." What had the GI who lost the comb been facing?

Moving on, past the few shattered, burned stumps of the old forest, we came to the edge of the replanted forest, the trees of which are now thirty to forty feet high. Half in the pines and half in the clearing, we found a square log-walled pit about three feet deep.

Trent held back the interlocking pine branches while I ran the metal detector head along the ground. Immediately the detector began buzzing loudly. I outlined a long narrow object. Another submachine gun?

After removing about six inches of top soil and roots, we uncovered a metal tube. It was a Panzerfaust, the one-shot bazooka developed by the Germans during the war. So now we know what the GI who had lost the comb had been facing.

The Panzerfaust lay near the rear of the pit, and it too was rusted although not as badly as the weapon I had removed from Hill 407.

After a half-mile of searching, we turned back. It had taken us four hours and we wanted to be home before dark. On the way back to the car, the boys took turns using the metal detector and I dug the holes on every hit. Before our shovel broke (the third in a

(James C. Byrk Photo)

Remnants of World War II discovered on the Siegfried Line.

month), we found more small arms ammunition and an empty U.S. hand grenade.

I'm still lacking a helmet for my collection of Siegfried Line souvenirs and I intend to keep looking until I find one. However, I recently made another discovery about the Bitburg-Trier area: it is famous for its Roman artifacts.

Some of the local residents told me of Roman coins found in the area, and some now in the State Museum in Cologne were found several years ago in Minden, only a mile from my home.

I am learning German and a colleague of my teacher's is a treasure hunter. Every summer I'm told he wades neck deep in the Mosel River at Trier, dragging a seive through the mud. He is well rewarded for his efforts with Roman coins.

It looks as though I'm going to have to break out my wet suit and learn to use my detector in water.

24
"Treasure" Island
by William F. Adams

Author's note: Before Dick and I asked Bill to write this chapter, we had never met him. We knew him by reputation as one of the top Civil War artifact hunters in the South. (So as not to confuse any of our readers, we must explain that Bill is from Atlanta and refers to that historical conflict as the War between the States.) Like Jim Walker, Jim Byrk, and Dave Radcliffe (Chapter 25), Bill has turned an interest in history into field experience, so that over the years he has become an expert in that area of the past. He is part-owner of Adams Explosives, which is in the rugged business of transporting dynamite, electric blasting caps, and other blasting supplies in Georgia. The firm also handles the loading and firing of these products.

• • •

Twenty years ago, a friend got me interested in searching for artifacts from the War between the States. We have been after them ever since.

In Georgia, Florida, Alabama, Mississippi, Missouri, Tennessee, North and South Carolina, Virginia, Louisiana, Illinois, and Washington, D.C., research has led us on a merry and sometimes sticky chase for "treasure."

It's a matter of search-and-find before other hunters unearth a virgin area. And that's not always easy. When you do, you sometimes find yourself knee-deep in a messy situation as we did at Black Island.

(Photo supplied by Bill Adams)

Bill Adams with some of his Civil War artifacts.

Black Island is off the coast of South Carolina near Charleston. Yankees were stationed there in 1863-64 to keep Confederate forces bottled up in Charleston harbor. I learned about the place when Tom Dickey[1] called and described it to me. He said that we had a good chance at being the first relic hunters to explore the island.

The island is in the center of tidal flats. During the 1860s, there were causeways between the islands to make easy movement possible. We would have no such access.

So the first thing we had to do was secure a boat to study the tide flow for that part of the coast. If the tide happened to shift on us, we would be caught in a very mucky situation — which is exactly what happened.

However, that was on a subsequent trip after we knew better. On

1. Tom Dickey is the author of *Field Artillery of the War Between the States* and *Siege Artillery of the War Between the States.*

the first venture onto the island, we played it pretty tight to the chest.

We found that the only access to the island was during high tide; when the tide was out, there would be no way of getting to shore again until the water rose twelve hours later.

With planning and luck, we decided we could get a carload of artifacts in the time we had. Obviously, we are optimists, but I'll let you find that out for yourselves. Read on.

Assembling maps and records, we discovered that there had been an assortment of Union troops stationed on Black Island. And from time to time they had exchanged artillery fire with Confederate forces occupying Charleston.

It looked like a big project, and we decided to take a large party. Friends with a boat in North Carolina were contacted. They agreed to meet us and take part in our expedition. Then we enlisted three other relic hunters from the Atlanta area. There would be seven of us searching.

The next week was spent in planning. We didn't want to leave anything undone, un-thought of, un-anything. We followed the weather like race track touts. Bad weather could mean a bad hunt. It was January and we were gambling.

We arrived at the site at night and started out the next morning. The weather seemed perfect.

Once in the water, Tom Dickey guided the party through a maze of canal channels. The island is about two and one-half miles from the nearest launching site.

As we moved between the little clumps of marsh grass on each side of the channel, the man at the wheel worked to keep us from running aground on the oyster bars. The sun was bright, yet it was a little cold and the spray from the bow felt like an icy mist on our faces.

After a quick search we knew that there was no channel directly to the island. We were going to have to wade through knee-deep water and fluff mud to get to high ground. Fluff mud sticks like glue to anything it touches when wet. When dry, it is extremely difficult to remove.

At what Tom determined to be the closest point to the island, we started to unload. I stepped out into a soft spot in the marsh grass and sank up to my knees. Of the seven of us, only two had the foresight to bring hip waders.

In spite of difficulties, we managed to carry our equipement to a central spot on the island. Before leaving the boat we secured it. By this time the tide was beginning to recede.

For the next twelve hours we would be marooned in a vast expanse of fluff mud. There is something disconcerting about being surrounded by a sea of ooze. The mind will play nasty little tricks on you such as: What if the tide doesn't return?

In treasure hunting under conditions such as these, it's important that you carry everything needed for that period of time during which you are stranded. In addition to our equipment, we brought along plenty of food and water, and a first-aid kit.

After setting up camp, we split up into parties of one and two. A companion and I worked the north side of the island and immediately began getting readings on our metal detectors. We found 69 caliber minnies and some smaller bullets. Then I found a bayonet scabbard tip and an unfired Spencer cartridge, which in my kind of hunting is a good find. The Spencer rifle was one of the reasons the Yankees won the war. It was a seven-shot repeater and could be fired between forty and fifty times a minute.

A short time later, we uncovered several eagle buttons, which had come off the uniform of a Union enlisted man. To those who think that this kind of "treasure hunting" is economically trivial, let me assure you, it isn't. Recently, items such as buckles from Union uniforms have been selling for $35 each; Confederates for $250 each. In one instance, one Confederate buckle sold for $2,100.

After an hour or so we paused in our search to discuss a plan of action. Since we had split up, we had not seen anyone from the rest of the group. But that wasn't surprising. The island, which is only a half-mile by a half-mile, is made up of a series of long, high points with swampy separations in between each one. Our people could be behind any one of perhaps eight hills.

We also discussed the possibility of snakes. We decided it.was too cold and immediately spotted one about two feet long. It looked like a water snake, so we threw it into the water.

When we returned to camp for lunch, we discovered that two of our colleagues had had a field day nearby. Included in their collection was a Spanish coin (circa the early 1800s), as well as several rings, an assortment of buttons, and about 200 bullets. But the prize was a VMM (Volunteer Maine Militia) buckle, which still had on it one of its two hooks. It would bring as much as $250.

Unfortunately, the man who found it had cut it when digging it up. It was a hard lesson and we all learned from it. The piece was still good, but it would have been perfect.

After lunch, Tom and his son, Tom, Jr., set off in search of a Hale's Rocket, a missile used by Union forces in this area. Others went in other directions. I headed for the area where the VMM buckle was uncovered. If there was one, there might be more.

It was a swampy area, but as soon as I began hunting, I was finding carved bullets. This indicated a place where soldiers had been camped for some time. They would carve bullets into chessmen and other interesting figures to pass the time. I felt I was in the right area.

Then I began finding Eagle I buttons. (The "I" stands for infantry.) I had been hunting about an hour when the signal in my earphones almost knocked my head off. It was so loud that I figured it to be a tin can, but I was taking no chances.

The signal was at a tree and I dug down at the base and uncovered a buckle. Holding it in my hands, I let out a whoop. It was covered with dirt so I washed the face with water from my canteen. When the letters VMM appeared, I must have yelled again because the head of one of my colleagues who was hunting nearby popped up.

I told him what I had found and went back to work. Quickly I found a couple of buttons and a bayonet scabbard tip and then I got another loud reading. Carefully, I dug until I uncovered the corner of another buckle. Then I stopped. Don't ask me why exactly. Maybe I really did need a drink of water. Whether I did or not, I sat sipping the water, looking at the corner of that buckle. When I finally did dig it up, it turned out to be my second VMM. I was ten feet tall.

Both were dug up near trees less than thirty feet apart. Their

Tom Dickie points out a Civil War projectile he uncovered.

distance from each other points out an important lesson for a beginning relic hunter. He has to search slowly, overlapping his steps. Anything small should be found that way. Anything large will take care of itself.

Other things were found before we left the island, but nothing of real consequence. By the time the tide was up, the sun was setting and the trip back was chilly.

Because of the tide factor, we picked easier places to get to the following day. Mostly we found junk, but Tom unearthed a monster of a projectile. The shell was a 200-pound Parrot that had been fired at a Confederate fort from a Yankee gunboat. Tom figured that the Parrot had hit the fort butt first. It was about thirty inches deep when he found it.

For Tom and me this turned out to be a good trip, but we are not always so successful, However, we enjoy what we do. We like to feel that we are in that group of relic hunters who have, through their own expense, time, and research, preserved countless artifacts from the Civil War era. It's our way of filling in the little gaps in history. For people like Tom, it is a way of passing on, through books, material and facts that might have otherwise been forgotten.

25
The Organized Treasure
Hunter
by Dave Radcliffe

Author's note: Most of us involved in metal detecting have an affinity for things past, if for no other reason than we like old money. But a love of history seems to rub off on us. Perhaps it's because we often touch things that no other man may have seen or held in his hands for hundreds, maybe thousands of years. Frequently we do our historical groping in an unorganized way. This is not the case with Dave Radcliffe, who has family ties with Zachary Taylor and Jefferson Davis. Dave, an independent communications consultant, is one of those efficient people who goes about his hobby of successfully seeking out Civil War artifacts in a very precise manner. His chapter, which may seem parochial at first, since it is confined to Missouri, demonstrates how artifact hunting should be done. However, he is simply supplying a foundation that could be applied anywhere. After all, the value of artifacts often depends on the story that goes with them.

● ● ●

Missouri is a state with fertile valleys, rich bottom land, and old mountains. Some geologists claim that when the waters that covered the earth eons ago subsided, the first piece of land to pierce the surface was Shepard Mountain in Missouri.

In this soil are buried the bones of mastodons. In this ground, minerals of every kind are found: silver, gold, tungsten, copper, barite, lead, and iron, among others. This is the cave state. There are more than 1,200 known caves in Missouri, of which 150 were found within the last twenty years.

These caves sheltered ancient man, mound builders, plains Indians, raiders, settlers, and even served as the first breweries west of the Mississippi.

Spanish conquistadors were marching through Missouri in the 1600s. In the 1700s, French, English, and Spanish explorers, American colonists, and bewildered Indians were all vying for the area.

Daniel Boone settled here as a Spanish governor, Lewis and Clark poled their way up the Big Muddy, Ulysses S. Grant lived here, Tom Sawyer and Huckleberry Finn were conceived here by Mark Twain. Blackhawk, the famous Indian chief, is buried under a downtown street in St. Louis. The turbulent mountain men outfitted themselves here.

In the 1800s, Missouri became a state. In the 1850s, it was

Dave Radcliffe with some of his Civil War souvenirs.   (Dick Richmond Photo)

fighting border wars with Kansas Jayhawkers, conflicts that eventually led into the Civil War, which divided Missouri as well as the nation.

Between the state militia, the regular army units, the soldiers of the Confederacy, and the guerrillas who actually fought against them all, Missouri was able to place third in the number of Civil War engagements fought within a state. Only Virginia and Tennessee posted more battles during the war.

It was in these conflicts that a number of legendary figures emerged: John Brown, William Quantrill, Belle Star, Frank and Jesse James, Coleman and Jim Younger, Bloody Bill Anderson, Archie Clement, Wild Bill Hickok, and others. Many later moved on to the new West, but they passed through Missouri first, and most left their mark on the state and its history.

Many stories can be told about the people and happenings in Missouri. However, this book is neither large enough, nor is it for that purpose that it is being written. The names are brought up only to demonstrate its long history and to suggest that, during the Civil War, Missouri was suffering a war within a war.

There are many artifacts still here, and with research and zeal the treasure hunter can have himself a field day. I will not attempt to list the many folktales of treasures lost or treasures to be found. What follows is basically a short history of the war and the locations and dates of the major battles in Missouri.

In 1861, the Missouri government was basically pro-South but claimed to be neutral. This neutrality ended May 10, 1861, when the State Militia at Camp Jackson (located at what is now Grand Boulevard and Olive Street in St. Louis) was surrounded by a large force of Missouri Home Guard, organized and mustered into service only three days earlier. There troops were mostly European immigrants who had served in the armies of Europe. They were commanded by Captain Nathaniel Lyon (later to become a general and die at Wilson's Creek).

The Home Guard forced the surrender of Camp Jackson without a shot, but on marching the prisoners to the Federal Arsenal, a mob sympathetic to the militiamen rioted, which resulted in the death of twenty-eight persons, among them women and children.

The aggressive and positive actions of Captain Lyon saved the arsenal and possibly St. Louis itself from the Confederacy.

The governor, Claiborne Jackson, a secret secessionist, made another attempt at foiling Lyon. In a meeting with Lyon (who was promoted by then to brigadier general because of his actions at Camp Jackson), he proposed that Missouri would remain neutral and would disband the militia if Lyon would refrain from enlisting Missourians into the Union army and moving troops through the state. Lyon's response set the tone for the war in Missouri.

His reply was basically that "before the United States government would concede to such an arrangement, he would see Jackson and every single man, woman, and child in the state dead and buried."

Civil rights were virtually suspended in Missouri, and with the loss of those rights and such statements as made by Lyon, many Missourians became "Missouri Confederates." They would not fight in the armies of the South nor outside the borders of Missouri, but they would and did fight as organized guerrillas in the state and probably caused more grief and expense to the Union than a regular force of Confederate troops could have done.

As a result, several hundred towns and hamlets in the state were attacked or raided by Missourians themselves. So for every battle listed in this chapter, there are dozens of others not listed. Hundreds of Missouri towns today can be checked over by the artifact hunter and his finds will give mute evidence to this fact. This, of course, can be extended to other states, but not with the same peculiarity.

The first shots were fired May 10, 1861, and the last of major importance during the war years was in October of 1864. Guerrillas such as the James and the Younger boys kept fighting until the last of the "Missouri Confederates" grew too old to care or were killed because they couldn't change a war that had changed them.

The major Civil War battles in Missouri are listed in chronological order. After each battle is an alphabetical designation that tells the artifact hunter if the site can be hunted or, if not, why.

(A)   Not worthwhile. Designates that community or town has been built over actual site, and evidence of the battle is probably concrete or fill.

(B)   Areas in and around are available for hunting. Research and get permission before searching.

(B*)   Favorable for artifact hunters. Permission usually not difficult and area does have relics.

(C)   Battle was actually fought over several miles with miscellaneous engagements. At some engagement sites, hunting favorable. At other sites, impossible.

(D)   Federal park—metal detectors not allowed.

(D*)   Not all of battle or staging area in the park. Parts on private property—get permission.

(E)   State park—metal detectors not allowed.

(E*)   Not all of battle or staging areas in the park. Surrounding area can be hunted with permission.

(F)   Some of battle sites in city parks—can be hunted.

(G)   Across river from Belmont in Kentucky is a Confederate fort. In state park—no hunting there.

NAME OF BATTLE		DATE
Seizure of U.S. Arsenal at Liberty	(A)	4/20/1861
Camp Jackson, St. Louis	(A)	5/10
St. Louis, Street Riot	(A)	5/11
Boonville	(B*)	6/17
Independence	(B)	6/17
Farmington	(B)	7/4
Carthage	(C)	7/5
Neosho	(A)	7/5
Athens	(B)	8/5
Potosi	(B)	8/10
Springfield	(A)	8/10
Wilson's Creek	(D*)	8/10
Birds Point, or Charleston	(B)	8/19
Lexington	(E) (E*)	8/29
Lexington, surrender of, by Union force	(E) (E*)	9/20
Osceola, destruction of	(B)	9/22
Charleston, expedition from, to Birds Point	(B)	10/2

NAME OF BATTLE		DATE
Belmont	(B) (G)	11/7
Warsaw, destruction of U.S. stores	(B) (F)	11/21
Charleston	(B)	12/12
Mount Zion Church, Boone County	(B)	12/28
New Madrid, siege	(A) (B)	3/3
New Madrid, capture of	(A) (B)	3/3
Clinton	(B)	3/30
Doniphan	(B)	4/1
Jackson	(B)	4/9
Bloomfield	(B)	5/10
Florida, Salt River	(B)	5/31
Lotspeich Farm, near Wadesburg	(B)	7/9/1862
Moore's Mill, near Fulton	(B)	7/24
Kirksville	(A) (B)	8/6
Newtonia	(B*)	8/8
Independence, surrender of Union forces	(A)	8/8
Lone Jack	(B*)	8/14
Lamar	(B)	8/24
Ozark, captured by Confederate troops	(B)	1/7/1863
Springfield, at and near	(A) (B)	1/8
Hartville	(B)	1/11
Bloomfield	(B)	1/27
Bloomfield, near, and capture of by Union forces	(B)	3/1
Fredericktown	(B)	4/22
Cape Girardeau	(A) (B)	4/26
Jackson	(B)	4/26
Sibley, destruction of	(B)	6/23
Marshall	(B)	7/28
Boonville	(B)	10/11
Lamar, destruction of, by Confederates	(B)	5/28/1864
Laclede, descent on	(B)	6/17

NAME OF BATTLE		DATE
Fayette, near and at	(B)	7/1
Camden Point	(B)	7/13
Versailles	(B)	7/13
Hunstville, attack on	(B)	7/15
Arrow Rock, attack on	(B)	7/20
Plattsburg, attack on	(B)	7/21
Shelbina, attack on	(B)	7/26
Rocheport, near	(B)	8/20
Steelville	(B)	8/31
Tipton, attack on	(B)	9/1
Centralia, at or near	(B)	9/7
Doniphan	(B)	9/19
Keytesville, surrender of	(B)	9/20
Patterson	(B*)	9/22
Farmington	(B)	9/24
Fayette, attack on	(B)	9/24
Jackson	(B)	9/24
Arcadia Valley	(B) (E*)	9/26/1864
Ironton	(B) (E*)	9/26
Shut-In Gap	(B) (E*)	9/26
Arcadia	(B) (E*)	9/27
Centralia	(B)	9/27
Fort Davidson, Pilot Knob, attack on	(E) (E*)	9/27
Mineral Point	(A)	9/27
Franklin (Pacific)	(A)	10/1
Union	(A)	10/1
Washington, occupied by Confederates	(A)	10/2
Osage River	(B)	10/5
Jefferson City, at or near	(B)	10/7
Moreau Creek	(B)	10/7
Boonville, at and near	(B)	10/9
California	(B)	10/9
Danville, attack on	(B)	10/14

NAME OF BATTLE		DATE
Glasgow	(B)	10/15
Paris, surrender of	(B)	10/15
Sedalia	(B)	10/15
Carrollton, surrender of, by Union	(B)	10/17
Big Blue, or Byrams Ford	(A) (F)	10/22, 10/23
Westport	(A) (F)	10/23
Charlot, or Marmiton	(B)	10/25
Clinton, attack on	(B)	10/25
Newtonia	(B*)	10/28

The artifacts of war are there, but with war come the side things such as people hastily burying their money before an attack by guerrillas. Throughout this state that was so ripped by conflict are the real treasures that Roy Volker and Dick Richmond are writing about.

It's a matter of seeking them out.

A super find that turned out to be a dud. This replica of a Confederate half-dollar was found in Richmond's house. On the other side is a "T" stamped next to the date, which indicates that it is a token.

(Dick Richmond Photo)

26
River Treasure

After all the years that Dick and I have been searching the ocean for sunken treasure wrecks, we may have stumbled upon one in our own backyard — in the Missouri River near Hermann.

In the spring of 1973, flood waters caused widespread damage up and down the Mississippi River and its tributaries, including the Missouri. The Big Muddy flooded over its banks and in several places had broken through its levees. When the water finally subsided, the Army Corps of Engineers got busy repairing the damaged dikes.

Dredges were put to work sucking sand from the river bottom to mend the breaks. In one case, Spanish and American coins (circa 1790-1820) were sucked out along with the sand and wound up in the levee.

They could have gone unnoticed and almost did except one of the workers happened to accidentally kick a Spanish silver dollar from the sand with his boot. He showed it to everyone, including a co-worker, Gary Gooch.

Gary, who had been on the dredge, got to thinking about where that coin might have come from. Then, as luck would have it, he found one. too.

However, he was tight-lipped about his discovery. Instead of displaying his coin, he returned to the site on his day off with a metal detector and found coin after coin on top of the dike just beneath the surface.

The coins were all in mint condition. Some were discolored from

117

(Dick Richmond Photo)

Gary Gooch in front of the levee in which he uncovered the Spanish and United States coins.

being in water. Others were as bright and shiny as if they had been sealed in plastic for all these years.

Gary's detector wasn't a very good one, and he came to me for a better one. He needed more penetration. He showed me the coins and told me the story. I felt they had to come from a wreck and asked him to take me to the site with him.

Naturally he was reluctant and at first refused. I explained with the electronics that I could perhaps locate a cache that might otherwise go undetected. At the time, Dick and I had not figured out how the coins came to be in the levee.

Despite my arguments, Gary refused. A week later he was back, unsuccessful in finding more, and agreed to take me with him. Another week passed before we were able to go to the site. It was during that week that luck turned away from Gary. More than two feet of earth was pushed over the sand.

One look and I knew we were in for trouble, but we searched regardless. For an entire day's work, we found just one Spanish bit, one-fourth of a silver dollar. But at least I saw the situation and was able to report it to Dick.

● ● ●

Roy and I came to the same conclusion. The coins had been sucked out of the river. We just didn't know how at the time. But it was enough for me to start researching. Looking for treasure wrecks on the rivers had never occurred to us before. It opened new vistas.

I visited the Army Corps of Engineers in St. Louis to find out what is required by them, since the river is a navigable body of water and is therefore federally controlled. That part of the river is under the

Gary Gooch (left) and Volker at the Missouri River where Gooch worked on a dredge that sucked late eighteenth- and early nineteenth-century Spanish coins and early nineteenth-century United States coins from the river bottom.

(Dick Richmond Photos)

control of the Kansas City division of the Corps, but I was told that a salvage permit was easy to obtain and given literature regarding working on the river. The office was very helpful and went out of its way to explain its position.

Don Paule went to the Missouri Historical Society to dig out information on river wrecks and then drove to Hermann to conduct interviews and see what information he could obtain from the town's libraries and historical societies.

I contacted the Missouri Geological Survey to see if I could discover how much the river channel had changed over the last 150 years.

We were getting some hot leads even before we were sure of what we were doing. There were scores of boats that had gone down nearby. Any one of them could be our wreck. One in particular, the *Boreas #2*, was very interesting. It had burned and had gone down with Spanish bullion aboard. There was scandal connected with its sinking. It was thought that the fire had been purposely set and that the silver had been removed before it caught fire.

That was the speculation at the time, and it very well may have been true. But it went down in 1846, which put it in the right time period, and at least gave us a foundation on which to base a search. We knew for sure that Spanish silver was being shipped up the river in bulk.

Roy and I had already started thinking about doing this book, and I was particularly anxious to include this in it. However, like everything else in the treasure-hunting business, frustration is something that one has to learn to live with.

• • •

It wasn't difficult to convince Gary to let Dick visit the site with us after the earth had been bulldozed over the top of the dike. I think he guessed that his chances of finding any more coins were pretty remote. But then for several weekends in a row we were hit with bad weather. When spring finally did arrive, Gary was working weekends repairing dikes south of St. Louis near Chester, Illinois. He couldn't make it, and we didn't want to go without him. After all, it was his find, and we were not about to jump his claim.

Some of the Spanish coins found at the levee at the site of the Missouri River "wreck."

(Dick Richmond Photo)

Bright weekend after bright weekend passed and still Gary couldn't make it. He kept insisting that we go ourselves. Dick was hesitant; he wanted Gary there to tell us exactly how the coins came to be in the levee. Finally one spring Saturday we did go without Gary.

• • •

Roy and I drove on the dike almost a half-mile before we came to the area where the break had been. There were two bulldozers working there yet, pushing earth up against the levee, which still wasn't completely repaired. To reach the area where Roy and Gary had found the bit on their last outing, we had to walk another three hundred yards.

A swath a hundred feet wide had been cut through the forest

(Dick Richmond Photo)

One way to get a half-dollar years ago was to cut a dollar in two. These coins were found in the levee at the site of the Missouri River "wreck."

between the river and the levee. On our next visit there, Gary explained what had been done.

At this particular point, the levee is a thousand feet from the river. A wide path had been cleared here to accommodate a large pipe that was carrying the sand being sucked from the river bottom.

The dredge, he explained, had anchored in the main channel with its back to the current. On the front of the dredge was a flexible pipe 100 feet long that swept the bottom like a vacuum cleaner or an air lift. When the pipe reached its maximum depth, the dredge was anchored a short distance downstream. This continued until there was enough sand to repair the levee.

But Roy and I didn't know this the first time we went up there. All we could do was guess, and in some instances we guessed wrong.

To me, it was all interesting hypothesis since, unlike Roy, I had not seen any tangible evidence of anything yet. We went to the levee to run our metal detectors across it. We knew it was foolish to work

Some of the United States coins found in the levee at the site of the Missouri River "wreck."
(Dick Richmond Photo)

(Dick Richmond Photo)

This gold stick pin was found by Volker and Richmond on the levee at the site of the Missouri River "wreck."

the top, but we did it regardless just to satisfy our curiosity. I found an empty cigarette package.

The river side of the levee was just as hopeless, so we worked the other side, which had not been covered by earth.

Morning passed into afternoon . . .

• • •

. . . and afternoon was starting to get hot and hopeless. I could sense Dick was pretty disgusted. I watched him pick up an occasional piece of metal and throw it out of our field of search.

I had hit nothing and occasionally would throw a quarter to the ground just to make sure my detector was working properly. It was; I just wasn't hitting anything.

Then I got a blip and saw the point of a gold pin sticking out of

the ground. I dropped to my knees and scooped out of the sand a
gold tie pin with a carved snake. Dick, who was working 100 feet
west of me, was over before I finished waving.

Five minutes later I found a well-used 1820 dime, and a minute
after that a brand new 1810 American half-dollar.

● ● ●

That was all Roy and I were to find the rest of the day, or at all,
for that matter. But that was enough, that and the coins Gary
showed us, to convince me that we had indeed stumbled upon
something.

Now we're waiting for the river to go down so Roy can use his
magnetometer and see if he can locate the wreck, if there is one.
The reason we think it might be one is that, in all our searching, we
found no remnants of a wreck. And we know the dredge could have
sucked parts of it up. It sucked a 400-pound boulder out of the
river. The boulder got caught in the pipe and Gary was part of the
crew that had to remove it.

If there is no wreck, and it seems incredible that the levee
happened to break just where money sometime in the past happened to fall off a boat, then the treasure that exists is all in a large
mound of earth and sand that is protecting a remote area of
Missouri countryside.

A Thank You Note

Besides those persons who were kind enough to contribute their talents in writing for this book, there were a number of others to whom we owe a great debt. Alphabetically: Robert C. Holt, Jr., Paul Kesterson, Carol Mainini, Don Paule, Art Phillips, Charlotte Richmond, Julius Schweich, Jr., Al Schweitzer, Susan Sicher, Bill Steele, Marge Volker, and Larry Williams. We hope we haven't forgotten anyone.

Property of.

James S. Porter

12551 Twintree Ln.

Garden Grove Ca